THE M[...]
O[...]
CHARISMATIC
HEALING

Teresa

May the peace of God
which is beyond our
utmost understanding
keep guard over your
heart & mind through
Christ Jesus.

THE MIRACLE OF CHARISMATIC HEALING

ANDY O'NEILL

MERCIER PRESS

MERCIER PRESS
PO Box 5, 5 French Church Steeet, Cork
16 Hume Street, Dublin 2

A CIP is available for this book from the British Library

ISBN 1 85635 136 X

10 9 8 7 6 5 4 3 2 1

To preserve the principles of confidentiality, names of persons in this book are fictitious, except where permission was specifically requested and granted to use them. Similarly some locations of stories are also changed.

Printed in Ireland by Colour Books Ltd.

CONTENTS

PROLOGUE

Even to the casual reader it will be plainly evident that each of my three previous books was written for different reasons. While the title of my first book, *The Power of Charismatic Healing (A Personal Account)* discloses the reason for its appearance, amazingly the stories of people, who on reading it had experiences of the widest variety, was the reason for the publication of my second book, *Charismatic Healing in the Modern World*. Finally the phenomenon of these happenings of a most unusual nature, surfacing constantly in the discipline so unexpectedly thrust upon me, prompted my friends in all walks of life and in many countries to canvass me to record these factual events. Hence the reason for the publication of my third book, *Charismatic Healing in Everyday Life*.

In 1995, an entirely new set of reasons dictated that my fourth book should see the light of day. The first of these considerations emerged as I was putting the finishing touches to my third book and it concerns the oldest problem in human history. My initial reaction was to decline the challenge it presented as it appeared ludicrous for me to even attempt to address this puzzle which has defied the wisdom of the ages. However, taking comfort in the old adage that 'even the cat can look at the queen', I concluded that I could at least sketchily outline this awesome conundrum and while accepting that in no way could I demystify it, I might at least assist in demolishing some of the considerable volume of waffle surrounding it. But I knew I just couldn't ignore it, as when it regularly presents itself to me through many people and situations, it then becomes much more than merely of academic interest. Should the subject under discussion in this paragraph still be a mystery to the reader, then there is no need to worry; it will clearly manifest itself as my book unfolds.

The second reason which compelled me to write this book concerns a world-wide phenomenon of gigantic proportions that wreaks awful havoc in the quality of human life. I have, maybe unscholarly, but very deliberately divided this subject into three parts because I believe it is not generally appreciated that all are inter-linked and inter-connected. Although I have seen success in the first and second stages of this condition, sadly I have never seen a miracle happen when this frightening affliction progresses to its third and ultimate destination. Frankly so far I have failed to find the key to the solution of this tragic condition through the Charismatic Renewal approach but maybe a fresh understanding of its first and penultimate stages may eventually prevent it from reaching its seemingly irreversible final state. Again purposefully I have not specifically identified this subject either, as I wish it to unfold gradually in the atmosphere hopefully generated by the recording in this account of so many healings ranging from the simple to the totally unexpected dazzling ones. After all, nothing succeeds like success so proceed in hope.

My third and final reason for writing this book is purely a simplification exercise aimed at removing forever for Christians, wholesale wrong thinking and false ideas, while endeavouring to replace these burdens with comfort, joy and relief for folk sincerely seeking to contact their Creator.

Needless to say, as one would expect, healing stories abound too in this work, healing which is as wide as life itself.

I make no apology either for the appearance of the word 'miracle' in the title of this book although it normally disturbs rationalists and even people who consider themselves conservative Christians. All I ask is that my work be read with an open mind. Then and only then, after calmly reviewing all the happenings described in the various chapters will it be possible to form an unbiased judgement. I am utterly confident that the verdict must then be that no word other than miracle could possibly explain these healings.

I invite you to come with me now, step out in expectant faith and walk on the waters towards the New Jerusalem. May the reading of this book bring healing of the mind, body and spirit to all who dip into it and may these miracles spread to loved ones and to every circumstance and situation that requires healing. Why not? Do not be afraid. Read on – in hope.

1

HEALING – AS WIDE
AS LIFE

One of the first scraps of basic knowledge projected to children in Christian homes and schools is the image that God is everywhere. But when little people grow up the myriad complexities, pressures and sheer pace of life conspire to push that childhood belief into near oblivion. However the very possibility of the existence of a Supreme Being, who always was, is, and forever will be, tends to confront many in adult life and in the most unlikely situations too. The truth of such an assertion could be confirmed by the experience of a middle-aged British medical practitioner on a flight from Florida to New York in the autumn of 1991. On board the plane with his wife and two teenage children, he found himself sitting with his son in a three-seater row while his wife and daughter were seated together much further down that jumbo jet. It was in these circumstances that I found myself sitting next to this father and son when three adjacent seats were unavailable on that flight for my wife Delia, our daughter Mary and myself.

After take-off, with seat belts unfastened, we introduced ourselves as I explained, we were returning to New York after enjoying sea, sun and sand on Miami Beach while I learned that this UK family were on their way home to London via the Big Apple, following a holiday in the Bahamas. When we ran out of conversation, my companions invited me to join them in Trivial Pursuit, but as there wasn't space to set up this world famous board game, we confined ourselves to using the question cards, each receiving a point for every correct answer. Imagine my surprise then when one of the questions posed to me was to name the UK city where a multi-national insurance company had its Head Office. Wasn't it the firm in which I had spent my entire working life! My new found friends were very amused when I explained how closely the question related to me, with the doctor exclaiming, 'What a coincidence! And you thousands of miles from that ancient city of Liverpool!'

Shortly afterwards our game had to be abandoned with the announcement that dinner was to be served. When the meal ended, the lights were lowered on this night flight and the doctor's son donned his radio head set, so his Dad, learning that I had retired, enquired how I was managing my new found freedom. When I revealed that strangely I had become a triple author, he was more than interested to hear my story. Actually, considering his profession, I was reluctant to name the subject-matter of my books, but as he persisted I disclosed that I wrote of my experiences of healing by the laying on of hands. To say that he was interested would be the under-statement of the decade as instantly he wished to know whether or not the discipline I referred to was part of or connected to alternative medicine. Finding my answer was in the negative, he quickly asked was I the seventh son of a seventh son, and learning I wasn't, enquired was this power to heal based on the 'mind over matter' technique. Hearing that I had no knowledge whatsoever of this discipline he next asked was I aware of anything in my personality or touch which might trigger off healing. Again I shook my head, affirming that I had no interest in such an approach. His inquisitiveness knew no bounds, I recognised, as he pressed me to outline the type and scope of the happenings I had recorded in my books so I described a few of these healings in various areas. Concerning physical cures the good doctor asked could these be classified as purely psychosomatic. I countered by first describing how a six month old baby, born with curvature of the spine was instantly healed by the laying on of hands, before asking him how such an event could possibly be explained away as a psychosomatic manifestation. He made no reply and although his veritable barrage of questions ceased he tried a new approach asking, 'Did you ever get yourself assessed?'

Utterly perplexed, I queried, 'Assessed by whom?'

'By a psychiatrist or a psychologist,' he explained.

Indignantly I exclaimed, 'You must be joking! Like everyone else I'm doing my best to keep out of the hands of the "head shrinkers"!'

My instant reaction brought a smile to him as he revealed, 'I'm a doctor of psychiatry'.

'Now you tell me!' I exploded.

However, in an effort to conclude his cross-examination I quietly testified as a Christian and Catholic, that when invited, I often lay hands on the sick seeking healing by the power of the Spirit of the Living God and His Word. My terse assertion caused my companion's mood to change, leading him calmly to declare, 'Andy, I was Catholic, but the day I left home at eighteen years of age I walked away from the faith simply because too much religion was pushed on me by my parents.' Very strangely he continued, 'I now live my life partly in the spirit of the parable of the talents by doing what I can for those around me with the skills I possess. But I'm certain when I die, then it's caput – oblivion. There is nothing after life on this earth.'

His no nonsense declaration of his philosophy provoked me to observe, 'Doctor, I hope you are wrong, but you can't hope I'm wrong.'

Instantly he sat bolt upright in his seat blurting out, 'Say that again!'

He had certainly heard it, but I repeated my observation word by word. However, seeing he was obviously disturbed I added, 'On the day you walked away from your faith, hope went with it, so on the one hand, when you come to die, you will sign off faithless without hope in anything or anybody. On the other hand when I die, my wish is to go out with Christian faith and in the hope of being surrounded by and recognising loved ones who have gone before me.'

As I refuse to enter into controversy or confrontation with those who oppose my faith, at this stage I excused myself to have a word with my wife and daughter, leaving a seemingly stunned psychiatrist staring unseeingly at the back of the seat ahead of him. On returning a quarter of an hour or so later I found the doctor and his wife sitting together, their son having gone to chat to his sister. I sat down and was immediately introduced to his good lady to hear her excitedly exclaim, 'Oh, I hear you have the gift of healing! Do tell me about it. It must be a very exciting lifestyle.' In no way did I want to cover that ground again; after all, I was on holiday, so I backed off, pleading, 'I've told my story to your husband; he can fill you in.' However, to avoid totally disappointing her, I scribbled on her dinner menu the titles of my three books with details of my publishers and their UK distributors. She took it gratefully. In an effort to finish this topic, I concluded, 'Anyway, you don't need to hear of healing. Aren't you married to a doctor?'

'Oh, if you only knew the healing we need for ourselves and our five children,' she replied, and to my astonishment she stretched out her hands, pleading, 'Please lay hands on me!'

In view of her husband's firm rejection of the Christian faith, naturally I hesitated, but in the spirit of 'in for a penny, in for a pound', I reached out my hands saying, 'Very well then, put your hands on mine'. She did so gladly. Next, in an effort to avoid any family discord or embarrassment I looked at her spouse and quietly asked, 'Would you care to join us?' Much to my amazement, he instantly and enthusiastically grabbed our hands, so I began the praising of God. I progressed then to quote from St Matthew's Gospel, chapter 8, verses 1–3, and from Psalm 91: 14–16, ending these scripture prayers by asking that the wish in Psalm 20, verse 4 be fulfilled in their lives. We finished this short impromptu prayer session by reciting the Lord's Prayer, Hail Mary and Gloria. Immediately our 'holy huddle' broke up when dramatically the over head seat lights flashed, 'Fasten your seat belts', as the captain of the aircraft announced we were about to land at La Guardia airport.

The time-honoured pre-landing hush descended on the passengers with each of the 360 souls aboard alone with their thoughts or maybe even with prayers. The lights of New York became clearly visible, the big plane seemed to drift lazily from the heavens towards the earth with the familiar thud of rubber meeting concrete, a welcoming sound signalling the resumption of conversation, as piped music reassured all aboard that the plane had landed safely. Seat belts were unfastened and the three of us shook hands, but the doctor's farewell request certainly surprised me as he enquired, 'Andy, you wouldn't have a copy of one of your books with you? I'd love to read it on the flight to London.' I couldn't facilitate him but his wife interjected, 'Don't worry. Andy. Both of us will be reading your books next week.' As I went in search of my family I couldn't help thinking that when travelling alone by plane, one has no choice whatsoever as to the type of fellow traveller one meets.

That night in New York, before I fell asleep in the city which boasts it never sleeps, I recalled my very strange meeting with that man on the flight. Was his atheism jolted, I wondered. Did he recall any of the words of prayers learned some 40 years previously? Did he recognise in himself anything at all of the innocence of childhood or did it occur to him that it might have been more than just a mere coincidence that he sat beside the only passenger out of the 360 on board who had written books whose subject-matter was the faith of his fathers which he had discarded four decades previously? Questions, questions. Finally before slumber's chains bound me, it amused me to realise that a practising psychiatrist had an unearthly experience; it all happened for him between Heaven and earth! Truly, the spirit blows where it wills.

Months later, when swimming in a heated pool in midwinter in Dublin, I recalled a memorable swim in the sea off Miami beach during the holiday there. It all happened quite simply when I elected to remain in the hotel complex in Florida on my own, when my wife and daughter went on a shopping expedition to town. I first took a book to the poolside and in a deck chair soaked up the sun for an hour prior to having a swim. However, before entering the pool, I looked over the retaining wall surrounding the hotel grounds and saw huge breakers rolling in on the adjacent beach. On the spur of the moment I opted for a swim in the sea, hopped over the wall and within seconds was in the surf. There I was, as happy as a kid at a circus, diving into the breakers and being carried in on the sand. Suddenly I became aware of a man standing at the water's edge who appeared to be keenly interested in my harmless frolicking in the waves so I eventually approached him and said, 'Hi! This is my first time here and the breakers are magnificent.'

He responded, 'You're enjoying yourself,' but cautioned, 'Do you realise you're at risk when you wade out above your knees?'

'At risk from what?' I enquired innocently.

'From shark attack,' he replied, authoritatively. Continuing, he explained, 'Don't let me put you off, but surely you must be aware that these are warm tropical seas. I often come here on holiday and last year I saw a wind-surfer killed by sharks and another man while swimming lost a leg.'

'Thanks for warning me, ' I responded, 'and you have certainly put me off!' He waved his acknowledgement and continued on his beach stroll.

It was only then that I took stock of my surroundings and although as far as the eye could see, people were walking in glorious sunshine on the seemingly endless stretch of sand, all were content to let the sea water cover their toes only. Realising I had failed to observe the travellers golden rule, 'When in Rome, do as the Romans do', I hastily retired to the hotel pool, considering myself to be fortunate to be still in one piece and alive to tell the tale. But as I had been enjoying my leisurely swim in the Dublin pool for 20 minutes, I ended my musings on past events, 'in far away places with strange sounding names', quit the pool, showered, dressed and headed for the exit of the sports complex. Walking past the reception area and realising that my annual subscription would be payable soon, I asked Alice, a receptionist whom I knew, for a bankers order form. Strangely, she opened her mouth but no sounds came, so grabbing a biro she scribbled, 'This morning, shortly after I came to work, I lost my voice', and then smiling handed me the form.

In an instinctive reaction I heard myself say, 'Alice, I have written three books on healing; you may or may not have heard of them.' In short, I explained, 'I lay hands on the sick and I see some remarkable results.' Unhesitatingly then and apparently with all the confidence in the world, I reached out

12

and with my thumb, put the sign of the cross gently on her throat saying, 'Be healed in the name of the Lord', before heading for the car park, leaving a wide-eyed receptionist staring uncomprehendingly after me.

Two days later I was surprised to see a letter from my sports club on their distinctive headed note paper; it was from Alice. The letter read:

Dear Mr O'Neill,
Within seconds of your departure from the Club on Friday afternoon last, my voice returned to normal.
I wish to thank you so much for your kindness.

Days later, on entering the club again, Alice, who was all smiles, rose to greet me. She seemed slightly in awe as she recounted being so stunned at the instant restoration of her voice; she rushed into an inner office and to all and sundry blurted out her extraordinary experience. Coincidentally, one of her fellow workers, Mary, commented that while she had read my books, she had never met me. 'Now,' Alice confided, 'both of us are planning to attend the prayer meeting in "Avila" next week.' I assured her that they would be very welcome, thanked her for her letter and headed for the pool area.

On the following Wednesday evening, as the crowds streamed out of 'Avila', Alice and her colleague Mary approached me. Mary, very contritely, said, 'I have a confession to make', and then revealed that although she thoroughly enjoyed my books, she was fully convinced that all who participated in the Charismatic Renewal Movement were 'religious freaks' who would be visited by men in white coats sooner or later! Furthermore because of these fears, she was always too scared to venture into 'Avila', but at Alice's pleading, agreed to accompany her. However, Mary had stipulated that both of them would sit as close to the door of the monastery church as possible in order to make a quick getaway should her worst fears be realised. Finally, with total honesty, Mary concluded, 'The people we surveyed in the church before the meeting seemed ridiculously normal but when I saw and heard the

Core Group I unequivocally admitted to Alice that their sheer normality, quiet conviction and common sense approach to things spiritual utterly demolished my fears, which I realise now were totally groundless.' Next, this lovely lady asked very sincerely, 'Please Mr O'Neill, will you pray with us?' I did so for all of half a minute, asking the Lord, from Psalm 20, that all their plans be successful with the desires of their hearts coming true too. Being aware that Alice and Mary were young, beautiful and unattached, I concluded my prayer by wishing that they would both enjoy in the future the happiness of married life. Hearing it, they left 'Avila' aglow; after all, I wasn't an insurance man all my working life for nothing!

Acknowledging that to enjoy a fulfilling lifestyle, it is absolutely necessary to constantly strive to achieve a correct balance of activities, therefore the last act of that Wednesday evening for me was given over entirely to pure pleasure. After spending some three hours at a prayer meeting it was with a clear conscience that I sat down at home to watch my favourite UK soccer team on television. As a veteran, I was instantly ushered into a veritable fairyland, enthralled with the skills of some of the world's top footballers as they played the game I love so well. If the old adage, 'All work and no play makes Jack a dull boy', is true, then surely it follows that all prayer and no fun would make Andy a dull guy! Anyway, the bottom line in the Good News business is it can never be successfully announced by dull evangelists!

As a minister of the Word, I am keenly aware of the seemingly ever-changing practices in the liturgy of my Church as it endeavours to minister to the needs of the flock in every age. Therefore, I deeply appreciate that the altar rails now no longer separate the clergy from God's people, a most welcome development removing forever the 'us' and 'them' stigma from Catholic Church services. In retrospect I gladly recall an incident on the occasion when a classmate of mine celebrated Mass while I acted as minister of the Word. Chatting together afterwards I light-heartedly remarked, 'John, you priests will have to look at your laurels, now that we lay folk are in the sanctuary.' He capped my observation beautifully by responding, 'Andy, I don't care where you operate, as long as you preserve your amateur status!'

For me, the liturgy revolves around the three major feasts – Christmas, Easter and Pentecost. I always associate joy with Christmas, holding that any Christian who is not joyful in the season when the Word made flesh is celebrated has never really understood or appreciated Christianity. Next, the spirit of the liturgy deepens at Easter, reflecting the awesome glory of God, a powerful sensation sharpened by the commemoration by the Church of Jesus Christ's passion and death, climaxing in Holy Week with the proclamation of the Resurrection on Easter Sunday. Actually since coming into the Charismatic Renewal movement I now realise to the full that the whole Christian faith depends on one happening – the Resurrection. Without belief in that one glorious event, Christ's horrible sufferings and undignified death would be both meaningless and senseless and would reduce Christianity to a sham. Furthermore any Christian who fails to strive to bask in that glory at Easter time can never have any comprehension of the depth of faith expressed in the closing words of the Gloria of the Mass – 'For you alone are the Holy One, You alone are the Lord, You alone are the Most High Jesus Christ with the Holy Spirit in the glory of God the Father'. Finally then my mood swings to wonder when the season of Pentecost arrives with the realisation that the complete story of the Redemption applies personally to me. By God's grace I now know I have been redeemed and can exult in the hope that an eternity of happiness is my destiny when life on this earth ends for me, as it surely will for everyone else too, Christian or otherwise. The whole implication of Pentecost then copper-fastens the astounding Good News, making it personal to me, emphasising the bottom line of all bottom lines in this life.

By God's grace then, since I have become involved with Renewal, naturally the feast of the Holy Spirit is of the utmost importance to me as in the riddle of the universe, I try to find the Lord in whatever spiritual life I may possess. In this context Pentecost Sunday in 1993 proved to be not a little significant when I attended Mass with my wife Delia. Minutes before

15

the Mass was due to begin it was discovered that the minister of the Word designated to attend had not appeared so I was pressed into service, accepting this last minute invitation on the grounds that my refusal would only compound the existing confusion. Consequently I had only time for a rapid glance at the readings and sequence, a classic example of speed reading under pressure!

Significantly, when the Mass leaflet was thrust into my hand, its masthead, 'Pentecost Sunday', in bold print seemed to leap out at me, producing a sensation of instant excitement, while I appreciated too that I was in the sanctuary participating so meaningfully in the celebration of the Eucharist surrounded by the Word. I was also conscious of a burning desire to perform well, knowing that, 'I was about my Father's business', spurred on by my belief that God is not honoured by inefficient, sloppy and lukewarm performances either in prayer or at work. Within moments it seemed the priest was inviting the congregation to sit back and listen to the Word so I walked to the podium and went into action, striving to send forth the readings to the best of my ability with every vestige of faith I possessed. Finally I invited the priest and congregation to join me in the reading of the sequence aloud and rejoiced as the whole church was filled with the sound of the voices of God's people, praising Him.

With my task completed I left the sanctuary, returned to Delia in the pew and stood to honour the Gospel satisfied, considering all the circumstances, that at least I didn't make a mess of things. With the Breaking of the Bread completed, we approached the altar and when the priest distributing Holy Communion stood before me, he placed the host in my hand as usual. Then to my amazement he held the fingers of my outstretched hand, paused and in a fairly audible voice said, 'Thanks for the beautiful reading'. Immediately, a unique sensation swept over my entire being and persisted long after I returned to our place in the pew and although I had received the host, meditative prayer was impossible for me at that moment. Basking in this new awareness or contemplative experience, whatever it was, I realised that I had now had some conception of the extraordinary transformation which occurred when the Holy Spirit descended in tongues of fire on the apostles, on the disciples and on Mary, the Mother of Jesus too on the first Pentecost Sunday. Furthermore, the experience absolutely confirmed that the Spirit blows where it wills, that men and women are composed of more than just body and mind and a walk with the Holy Spirit is certainly filled with pleasant surprises. I knew I had also seen fulfilled the promise that was contained in Isaiah chapter 55, verses 10–11, where we learn the awesome power released when the Word of God is sent forth. Undoubtedly that good priest had been affected by hearing the Word some fifteen minutes earlier, so much so that he took the opportunity to express his thanks to me and fairly publicly too. Shakespeare's beautiful thought concerning the quality of mercy which he compares to the gentle rain from Heaven blessing those who give and those who receive also applies when one person thanks another, I acknowledged. Jesus Christ thought so too, as St Luke describes in chapter 17, verses 1–19, of his Gospel where the Evangelist tells of a healing.

On the Wednesday evening following that Pentecost Sunday, at the laying on of hands after the prayer meeting in 'Avila', a middle-aged lady approached me; at first glance she seemed very confused. When I welcomed her, she told me that her name was Ann and she confided that she had had frightful pains for months past, with a condition that had defied the ministrations of her doctors. A neighbour had brought her to 'Avila' to seek healing but Ann disclosed that she had never heard of the Carmelite Monastery nor indeed had she any knowledge of the Charismatic Renewal movement either.

Ann explained, 'Although I have been at your meeting for the past hour and a half, in no way was it meaningful to me at all, as all I am conscious of is this awful throbbing, non-stop pain in my head.' Still confused, she asked, 'What have I got to do here in this room now?'

Quietly I explained I would lay my hands on her head and seek healing by the Word of God and by the power of His Holy Spirit, provided that she agreed. Ann consented with the air of one who just wanted this last act of the night over and done with so that she could return home. I placed my hands on her head, saying, 'Lord, You said, "Heal the sick", so please remove this pain from Ann, now, by Your power and Your glory.' I removed my hands and asked, 'Is the pain gone?'

She did not answer, but now looked more puzzled and shocked than confused. As she remained totally mute, I repeated my question but Ann, very unsure of herself, responded, 'I don't know!'

'Surely you must know,' I gently insisted, adding, 'Either the pain is still there or it has vanished'.

Next, a look of wonder spread over her features as she revealed the reason for her hesitancy, exclaiming, 'Oh God! The pain is gone!' while at the same time she became unsteady so I held her by the upper arms.

Realising that she had no knowledge of people resting in the Spirit, when she murmured, 'I think I'm going to collapse with the shock', immediately I cautioned, 'Listen Ann, we are much too busy here tonight and haven't the personnel nor the time to look after people lying on the floor!'

She reacted positively to my observation, confirming her instant cure, indicating that she was no longer wrapped up in her own problems by requesting healing for a sick grandchild! With her maternal instinct now so obviously visible, first I gave the glory to God for her healing before asking the Lord that her grandchild be set free from illness, whatever it was. Ann thanked me, now confident and serene as smiling, she gracefully withdrew.

Driving home, I reviewed that miracle of healing, concluding as surely as the Holy Spirit had so clearly indicated to me His presence at Mass on Pentecost Sunday, that happening had now been followed by the manifestation of His infinite healing power in the dramatic cure of Ann on the evening of the third day after my unique and very special personal experience. It was consoling to realise too that the claim that the second Pentecost is truly, vibrantly alive and well and living in the Charismatic Renewal movement in our day and age while startlingly confronting and contradicting atheists, agnostics, secular humanists and the indifferent, can hardly now be seriously disputed.

IN 'AVILA' ON WEDNESDAY evenings, 'those who have eyes to see' witness the spectacle of the whole Church in action in the modern world. Gathered there are priest and laity, male and female, young and old, sprung from numerous different backgrounds, sharing the one faith focusing on its centre-piece, Jesus Christ, 'the same yesterday, today and forever'. On that very special evening in their week, they leave all other activities to follow Him, while concentrating on the real purpose and aim of human existence – personal salvation. Realising that there is no real point or profit whatsoever in gaining the whole world should they suffer the loss of their eternal souls and accepting that, 'their lives flee like shadows before them', this Wednesday evening congregation sets about plotting that course by embarking on a fool-proof route towards that end. Primarily they honour their maker in a time-honoured and traditional way of worship by praising God aloud. They then hold a solemn ancient service of the laying on of hands to heal the sick by the power of the Holy Spirit, knowing sickness is universal. In such a programme they discover the whole law and the Prophets fulfilling the two great commandments of God, the love of the Lord, while serving the neighbour graciously for His sake. The Catholic Church by its very nature must always project a caring image; it has always done so unfailingly in ages past. Now, in this day and age, that same traditional role is faithfully preserved and continued in the Charismatic Renewal prayer meeting in 'Avila' and in every traditional orthodox Charismatic Renewal prayer meeting worldwide. This caring is visible and accessible at these gatherings, to the present generation who, because they are creatures of mind, body and spirit whether or not they know, deny or neglect it, still have an in-built desire to solve the riddle of existence. All the creature comforts in the world never have, can or will minister to the spirit within human beings, an observation copper-fastened by the old adage that while everyone born has the gift of life, each individual must discover the art of living.

By the power of the Holy Spirit, countless thousands world-wide during the last quarter of a century have been introduced to the fine art of living the full life through the Charismatic Renewal movement, a way of behaviour totally in conformity with modern living, unexpectedly revealing the spiritual dimension even in the most ordinary of mundane pursuits. Truly the various patterns of life have a much deeper significance than might appear on the surface, as many casual visitors to the 'Avila' Wednesday evening gatherings discover when they come to see signs and wonders and they experience a spiritual transformation. Even people who stumble across the Charismatic Renewal prayer meeting in 'Avila' realise that the Holy Spirit comes in various ways and to some when they least expect it, as the experience of one lady testifies.

Sister Mary was in her early fifties and a member of a semi-contemplative order since her mid-twenties. She never experienced any spiritual upheavals, her life running on an even keel. Her convent was in the north-west of Ireland and she arranged to come to 'Avila' for a ten day retreat in the summer of 1994. Sister Mary marvelled at the peace in the monastery grounds, considering it is sited within minutes of Dublin's city centre. One can imagine her confusion then when strolling in these normally quiet surroundings after dinner in the very early evening of her first Wednesday there when suddenly the whole place started to buzz as cars began to arrive. Within a short time the two car parks were filled while a constant stream of people headed for the church. Her confusion deepened when she heard next she heard songs of praise wafting on the humid summer air echoing softly round the entire surroundings, followed by a very strange plain chant-like mixture of instrumental and choral music. This new mysterious audibleness, to Sister Mary, began softly and rose to a crescendo before fading away gently and seemingly effortlessly, leaving silence to reign supreme once more.

Fired up with curiosity she hurriedly re-entered the monastery through the reception area to find the whole building alive with the sound of music. Just then, one of the

Carmelite monks was passing her in a corridor, so Sister Mary asked him what was happening and learned a Charismatic Renewal prayer meeting was in progress. The priest advised, 'Take a quick look at it; it is well worth a visit -- the Holy Spirit is there!' He spoke with such quiet authority that she immediately headed towards the church, on tiptoe. However, she was amazed to find that she could not gain entry as the meeting had attracted a full house, so she had to content herself with standing near one of the entrances where she listened for the first time to a Charismatic Renewal meeting in full flow, the whole experience filling her with a mixture of wonder and bewilderment.

When the meeting ended, Sister Mary next noticed people hurrying to one of the lecture halls, in the monastery, where they stood in a long orderly queue awaiting admission. There the ceremony of laying on of hands for healing was about to commence, she discovered. The whole occasion seemed to generate its own momentum she realised, astounded by the matter of fact acceptance by all present of such purely spiritual values. Ordinary lay people living in the world from which she had voluntarily withdrawn had administered a sudden sharp but not unpleasant shock to her. In no way though was her quota of surprises by the Holy Spirit filled for the evening, as, whilst leisurely walking to the dining-room for a night-cap of a cup of tea, she passed the book stall where a publication under the title *The Power of Charismatic Healing* brought her to an abrupt halt. She began to browse through it in wonder, bought it, instantly did a u-turn and headed for her room with all thoughts of liquid refreshment now vanished.

There, in bed, one day departed forever and three hours of the next day had actually passed without her being even remotely conscious of it. Reluctantly she eventually placed the book under the pillow and put out the light, and marvelling that for the first time in almost a year, hope had come with even a tiny prospect of peace visible in a particularly distressing situation concerning a member of her family.

Sister Mary was the eldest of six children, and because she delayed her entry into religious life until her mid-twenties, an almost mother and son relationship developed between her and Jack, the youngest of the clan. He was a fine sportsman and a brilliant academic who immediately after graduation joined one of the armed forces in the UK, attracted to the outdoor life, and its career prospects. Promotion came rapidly too but it did not curtail other pursuits in his life, one of whom was Laura! This raven-haired beauty came from a family steeped in Royal Navy service, a tradition unbroken for centuries, so when Jack and Laura met, they had a lot in common and quickly fell in love. It was a very happy marriage and they were blessed with two children, a boy and a girl which provoked Sister Mary to good-humouredly refer to Jack and his clan as a typical British Protestant family! However, she thanked God, though Laura was Lutheran, that she was warmly welcomed by Jack's parents and accepted by her in-laws while in turn Laura had no difficulty whatsoever with the children being raised Catholics. Frankly she declared that there were only two obstacles preventing her accepting the Catholic faith, and they were the transubstantiation and the Blessed Virgin Mary being proclaimed Mother of God. Even a close study of Vatican II documents with specific reference to Catholic Mariology failed to dispel her difficulties leading Jack to jokingly promise to some day enrol in a theology course in an endeavour to assist Laura in discovering the truth!

However, when their eldest son reached his seventh birthday, a marital storm broke in Jack's life with frightening rapidity when he returned home on leave after a three month stint abroad on a special assignment and found Laura very upset. For the first few days she refused to disclose even the slightest clue as to the cause of her discontent but then out of the blue informed him that as far as she was concerned the marriage was over! In her own words she 'wanted out'. In short, Laura was looking for a divorce, the demand leaving her husband shattered. She explained that there was no other man in her life and guaranteed Jack reasonable access to the children, her sole aim being to re-enter the commercial world as a divorced mother of two.

For Jack, the swiftness of the affair left him non-plussed, as

Laura steadfastly refused to consider counselling. Laura's parents were aghast at the news as were Jack's family, but his wife was adamant and within days of her announcement she had consulted a solicitor.

Sister Mary could hardly believe her ears when Jack rang with the news, but Laura rigorously pursued her goal and within twelve months of her initial disclosure that she wanted her freedom, Jack, to his dismay, found himself a divorcee. Sister Mary felt completely helpless and could see no avenue of hope when suddenly she was catapulted among people in 'Avila' at a Charismatic Renewal meeting who, when difficulties arose in their lives, stepped out in expectant faith and sought a miracle. On reading the record of signs, wonders and healing detailed in my third book, she accepted that followers of Jesus Christ had always lived with miracles as did the Jewish people from whom Jesus Christ sprung. Now Sister Mary asked me in a letter for prayers for the healing of Jack's marriage.

At this stage, by way of explanation, may I say I never intended to set up a 'dial a prayer' service, nor do I promote or practice it personally. Regarding prayer, I am firmly convinced my prayers are as effective or as ineffective as any other praying theist when judged by results in this life. There is a well known saying among betting people in horse racing circles – 'all punters are equal on the turf and under the turf'. Be that as it may, I know all Christians are equal before the Lord in this life. Jesus Christ came and redeemed all without exception while not denying people the free will to accept or reject that redemption, and hopefully, by God's grace, I will persevere in the acceptance of Him to the end of my days. However, as regards being equal, don't take my word for it; St Paul teaches in Galatians chapter 2, verse 6 that God has no favourites. Therefore there are no god-children, marginalised people, disenfranchised or handicapped people, nor VIPs either before the Creator. Whatever difference there is between people is merely one of function. In the context of this firm conviction then, when people contact me explaining their difficulties and seek prayer, first I recommend that they attend a weekly

Charismatic Renewal prayer meeting. Second, I suggest that they read a short passage of Scripture which I choose to suit their particular needs in the firm knowledge that the most powerful form of prayer is that based on the Word of the Living God. It must be so as Jesus Christ said that even should Heaven and earth pass away, His Word would not pass away, with the prologue to St John's Gospel confirming this eternal truth. Third, should the Charismatic Renewal way of worship be unfamiliar to enquirers, I point them to one or all of the three books where I unashamedly set out my stall. Finally I say a short prayer with them. After that I consider my job done, the ball is in their court with the rest up to them and the power of the Holy Spirit. At this stage I bale out, turn their needs over to the Lord and I don't expect them to contact me again unless they have a miracle to report, which thank God, is not seldom.

So too with Sister Mary, I respectfully acknowledged her letter, suggested she read daily the Prologue to St John's Gospel, recommended that she attend her nearest Charismatic Renewal meeting weekly to praise God there for the healing of Jack and Laura's marriage and added a short personal prayer for the situation. Finally to emphasise my conviction that all are equal before the Lord I advanced the view that when the Holy Church canonised people it might inadvertently have given the impression that the saints were so special that the rest of us counted for very little, which cannot be true. Why even in the parable of the Lord of the vineyard and the labourers, it is laid down that the first shall be last and the last shall be first. In that Scripture found in St Matthew's Gospel chapter 20, the employer asks, 'Cannot I do what I like with what I own?'

Sister Mary however wrote one final letter to me but could not agree with my approach. In no way, it appeared, could she personally pray in the spirit of 'with God nothing is impossible', nor apparently could she handle the Will of God syndrome either. For her, life seemed filled with cross carrying and strangely whether these came from God or were self-manufactured seemingly made no difference. As far as I could make out, she seemed blinkered by a crucifixion complex which left no room at all for the Resurrection, thereby in my estimation reducing Christianity to a most unattractive philosophy. Even the consoling, centuries old teaching of the Holy Church that among the first fruits of the Spirit are peace and joy seemed to affect her not at all. She made it perfectly plain that she wished to have nothing to do with the Charismatic Renewal way to the Lord and should I not be prepared to pray for Jack, then that was the end of the matter.

Rightly or wrongly I got the impression Sister Mary viewed prayer of petition as inferior to meditation or contemplative methods whereas my point of view is that prayer is prayer! Could it be the difference between the three dimensional forms of prayer is as thin as a razor's edge? 'By their fruits you shall know them', is a philosophy I accept, therefore by God's grace, when the Charismatic Renewal way of worship works for me, why would I change? Furthermore, I also know it is a waste of time and energy endeavouring to 'talk' people into Renewal or to argue with them. The spirit of Renewal is 'caught'; it can never be imposed nor taken by violence either. The Spirit blows where it wills, when it wills, on whom it wills and neither can it ever be programmed, manipulated or organised. People in Renewal are not better, more elitist or more important than other practising Christians, but they are different, being people of praise steeped in the Word of the Living God. As truly as Saul on the road to Damascus, muttering murderous threats against the first Christians, was poleaxed by the power of the Holy Spirit to be found three days later in that city proclaiming, 'Jesus is the Son of God', so too the same Spirit is more than capable of doing a similar job in the lives of Sister Mary, Jack, Laura and her family. Sister Mary received a number of surprises during her stay in 'Avila', when for a few fleeting hours, the darkness in the lives of four people dear to her was unexpectedly illuminated. By God's grace may a fresh chapter filled with good news be written in their life stories.

THE BASIC UNIT GROUP of society, as we know and understand it, is the family. It follows therefore should this unit be destroyed then chaos must inevitably result with some commentators going as far as to say, 'destroy the family and people will tear each other asunder like wild dogs'. Theists, those who believe a Supreme Being created the universe and all it contains, also believe that mankind was directed by that same creator, 'to increase and multiply and fill the earth', hence the presence of the basic urge or instinct in humans to reproduce themselves. It is also generally accepted that the most natural and best environment for the successful rearing of children is a permanent group presided over by a father and mother. Viewed objectively then despite declarations of some advocates of the feminist philosophy of the right of single women to motherhood, this principle must be classified as a direct attack on the family and therefore on society itself although it may be unintentional. Furthermore, in this day and age, the phenomenon of the widespread breakdown of marriage with the consequent universal introduction of divorce also brings an additional hazard to threaten the very existence of the traditional family, a fact which must be considered irrespective of one's view on divorce. All in all then it certainly is a very rough world in which to exist, for an incurable romantic like me! Should any reader be firmly convinced that romance is nothing more than a charade or a myth created and promoted by storytellers for the simple minded and the immature, then I would suggest that now is a good time to leave this chapter and proceed to the next one! But if romance turns you on (as it certainly turns me on!) then come with me and listen to true stories of how real people in today's world had their lifestyles radically and unexpectedly changed following involvement in the praising of God and his Holy Word.

Mary left school at eighteen and, unattracted to academic life, went straight to work, remaining with the same firm for some ten years or so. She thoroughly enjoyed her job in its personnel department and was making her mark in the business world, achieving significant promotion. I knew Mary socially for years and I recall meeting her one sunny Saturday June morning in Dublin's Grafton Street. She seemed highly excited, blurting out, 'Hi, Andy! Fancy meeting you here! But maybe it's a good time for me to say goodbye; I'm off to Java next week on a three year contract!'

Very surprised, I enquired, 'How did this come about?'

She explained quickly, 'Actually, I found myself in a rut in the job, so I looked around, saw this position advertised, applied for it and got it! I left my own firm as the challenge of working abroad and learning a new language appeals to me. Anyway, it might change my luck too', she concluded with a twinkle in her eye.

We shook hands and capturing her mood, I responded saying, 'The very best of luck Mary, and may the Lord bring a nice guy into your life', adding with a smile, 'maybe as nice as myself!' as I made the sign of the cross on the second finger of her left hand.

Mary's eyes opened wide in wonder as she delightedly exclaimed, 'Hey, Andy! What are you doing?'

'Don't laugh too loudly, Mary,' I cautioned. 'I've quite a good track record in this business. But the bad news is that I charge for this service – a slice of wedding cake!' Our laugh a minute casual meeting ended when I gave her a peck on the cheek as she waved goodbye, walking off with a spring in her step, heading for the Far East.

The following Christmas, among the cards we received was one with an unfamiliar post mark; it was from Java of all places. Wondering who would be contacting us from that part of the globe, opening the envelope, we found a state of the art Christmas card, hand painted, from our friend Mary. In a short note she described life among millions of people there, disclosing that in six months she had only met three English speaking people. One of these was a man her own age, also there on a short term work contract and wasn't he from a place called Dublin! They hit it off from the word go and then I could hardly believe what I was reading. Astonishingly her letter next gleefully recalled our meeting in June when our fun-filled farewell climaxed when I made the sign of the cross on her finger; now here she was announcing that she and her fellow Dubliner had fallen in love, had become engaged for Christmas and planned to return to Dublin the following June to marry in their native city! Mary finished her note asking me to look out for the slice of wedding cake! Just imagine, I reflected, two Dubliners had to travel to the ends of the earth to meet, fall in love and plan a June wedding in Dublin! Dwelling on the news from Mary's point of view I concluded 'Victory to the brave', with a little bit of help from the Holy Spirit, I conceded.

The next romantic tale concerns a thirty year-old New York girl, Hilary, who came to Ireland in the spring time, on holiday. It was her first visit to the land of her forefathers, and landing at Shannon Airport, she hired a car and headed for the west coast, complete with road map and an Irish Tourist Board holiday brochure. Early that same afternoon, Hilary came to a small quaint village in Clare and, seeking farmhouse accommodation, was immediately attracted to one establishment. This particular dwelling was fronted by a plant-filled conservatory, with the house surrounded on three sides by neatly fenced paddocks where cattle contentedly grazed. Crowning it all, however, was a simply magnificent vista of the North Atlantic wastes. Quite a change from Fifth Avenue, Broadway and the Bronx! The Yankee visitor was made very welcome by the lady of that house, and was thrilled when invited to join the family for their evening meal which began with grace devoutly recited in Irish. The whole setting was akin to a fairy-tale for Hilary as she relaxed in the conservatory after the meal, fascinated by the glorious spectacle as the sunset magically illuminated the rolling landscape while transforming the sea into a shimmering symphony of breathtaking colours. Next Hilary was ushered into the cosy sitting-room where round a blazing turf fire, two neighbours called and chatted of cattle, milk and fishing. The conversation then turned to religion and the Charismatic Renewal movement in particular and while Hilary was vaguely familiar with this topic she had little knowledge of it but was interested, being a practising Catholic. Strangely when bed-time arrived, her host casually handed her a book remarking, 'You might like to browse through this for a few minutes before going to sleep'. It was *The Power of Charismatic Healing* by you know who! Hilary had had a long day and looked forward to eight hours of uninterrupted dreamless sleep, but propped up in bed, decided to read a page or two of the book. Amazingly though it was almost three hours later when she finally put out the bedside lamp and slept the sleep of the just.

The following morning, the family, having scattered early, hastening to work and school, Hilary had breakfast alone with her host. There she unburdened herself, telling of her great longing to marry, possibly motivated by reading of the signs and wonders recorded in the book which had halved her normal night's sleep. Hearing this, her host surprisingly but very naturally said a very short prayer with her asking the Lord to grant Hilary the happiness of married life – and soon! Three weeks later, this US visitor walked into 'Avila' Dublin on a Wednesday evening to attend the Charismatic Renewal prayer meeting, now much more knowledgeable of the Renewal after reading my three books, and when the meeting ended, presented herself at the laying on of hands unashamedly asking for prayers for a suitable partner in marriage!

Obviously these prayers in two locations in Ireland were no hindrance either, as six months later, on a trans-Atlantic telephone call, a gracious farmer's wife in west Clare rejoiced as Hilary announced glad tidings – she had met a man, they fell in love, they were engaged and planning a Christmas wedding! She also disclosed that his name was Jonathan, a name meaning 'gift from God'. Consoling to know, isn't it, that despite all the startling changes in today's world, romance is still alive and well and living in places as far apart as New York and Java!

As the old song proclaims, love and marriage go together like a horse and carriage, so when courtship leads to marriage solemnised by a church ceremony and joyously consummated, the sense of unique pleasure with joy and solid satisfaction is commonplace. Nevertheless, some married couples, after two or three years together, discover a type of stress hitherto unknown by them when the prospect of infertility looms. Personally speaking, with our first child arriving twelve months after our marriage, I never even remotely realised the stress and strain endured by childless couples and I might never have been aware of it if I had not been so unexpectedly catapulted into the Healing Ministry of the Holy Church. In retrospect, I must have been a very 'laid back' type as the existence of this discipline never crossed my mind either!

The foregoing reflections on love and marriage were very familiar to Ursula and Albert who, living in the south-east of Ireland were alas childless after seven years of marriage. Despite the medical tests indicating that there was no deficiency on either side to prevent Ursula from conceiving, sadly it was just not happening. In these circumstances, a neighbour of theirs, Peggy, having read my books, contacted me via the Charismatic Renewal group in 'Avila', outlined Ursula and Albert's dilemma and sought prayers for the gift of a family for them. As is customary, Peggy and her two friends were pointed towards the nearest Renewal prayer meeting in their area of residence and also recommended to read daily from St John's Gospel, chapter 2, 'The Wedding at Cana in Galilee', so by praising the Lord and the power of the Word of the Living God, Ursula and Albert might be granted their heart's desire. I presume they accepted these recommendations and acted accordingly as Peggy maintained contact with me by letter and telephone for some months. However, the last episode in this saga was disclosed when a bulky postage packet from Peggy arrived at my home almost a year later. On opening it I rejoiced on reading the good news that Ursula and Albert were now proud parents of a bouncing baby boy confirmed by the enclosure – a beautifully decorated box containing a piece of the christening cake! Actually, I have placed that tiny box among my healing memorabilia for it symbolises the beginning of new life in the lives of Ursula and Albert.

To sum up then, while nobody or no discipline can heal everybody or everything those involved in the Charismatic Renewal prayer movement by endeavouring to remain true to their vocation as people of praise, by accepting Scripture as the basis of their spiritual lives and by continually laying hands on those seeking healing, constantly witness miracles. It can hardly be otherwise with an approach which honours the two great commandments of God while fulfilling the Lord's new commandment too. Irrespective of what sceptics think, Mary in Java and Hilary in New York will forever joyfully associate the Charismatic Renewal movement with the arrival of the loved ones to share their lives with while Ursula and Albert in Ireland also gladly acknowledge the awesome power of the praising of God with a much longed for child, transforming their lives. Maybe when The Beatles came up with the song title, *All You Need is Love*, they were closer to the eternal truth than they ever imagined!

2

Unmasking the World-wide Destroyer of the Quality of Life

Should a man from Mars find himself planted in the spacious grounds of 'Avila' Carmelite monastery, Dublin, early on a Wednesday evening his first impression of earth people would be that they move on foot and use various means of transport too. He would see many people walking, dismounting from bicycles, viewing motor cars bringing from one to six persons, mini buses bringing from sixteen individuals with occasionally buses each delivering some fifty or more passengers. Should he research further he would find that while these people had come from many parts of Dublin, others had taken hours to reach 'Avila' with a liberal sprinkling of visitors from overseas arriving too. This creature from outer space would also be very conscious of the prevailing sense of excitement generated by this gathering but hidden from him would be the almost infinite variety of reasons which motivated people to attend this particular venue.

Petra was one such bus passenger who on a Wednesday early in 1993 undertook a round trip of some 200 miles to participate in the prayer meeting in 'Avila'. She was involved in the Renewal movement in her home town and having read my books she hoped that her seriously ill sister would be healed when she praised God for her in one of the largest weekly meetings of its kind in the western world. Petra was very consoled by the warm greeting extended to her and her group, entered actively and enthusiastically into the very evident seven Charismatic ways of worship and presented herself, representing her sister, at the laying on of hands when the meeting ended. A week or so later, Petra rang me, introduced herself and on behalf of her group extended sincere appreciation of the welcome they received from the monks and people at 'Avila', which she said made their visit memorable. Next she maintained that the $2\frac{1}{2}$ hour journey had flown with the 52 strong party joyfully and spontaneously praising God in words, tongues and songs of praise. Then, Petra announced that she had heard a very strange sound during the journey, so, puzzled, I immediately asked, 'What kind of sound?'

She took a deep breath and then as cool as a breeze explained, 'Andy, while in no way am I deaf, I actually heard myself laughing!'

'For goodness' sake, what's so special about laughing?' I countered.

In reply, Petra revealed that when she laughed, she suddenly became aware of it, realising it must have been years since she had done so! She was also amazed at herself listening keenly to the laughter and good-humoured banter surrounding her, astounded that she had apparently conditioned herself for so long to reject and ignore all sounds of merriment. At the journey's end, Petra outlined how she was left at the door of her house in the early hours of Thursday morning, silently entered and retired to bed, quite astonished at being so light-hearted. Furthermore, she pointed out that without specifically seeking it, the gift of joy expressed in laughter returned to her after her praise and prayer session in 'Avila'. While acknowledging her afflicted sister had shown no sign of improvement, she calmly insisted that both of them were now full of hope, facing the future with complete trust in the providence of God. Concluding, Petra said, 'I must go now or I'll be late for work but I'm thoroughly enjoying myself, seeing what a startling effect my new personality is having on my family, on my colleagues at work and on my friends.'

The call ended with Petra's seemingly carefree wish, 'Good luck Andy, and God bless "Avila"'. Reflecting on Petra's story, whether or not in the jargon of Renewal she had a personal experience of the Lord, it goes without saying she certainly received the grace of self-awareness. Although she may have never read the spiritual advice of St Teresa of Avila – 'Don't take yourself seriously; take God seriously' – in effect Petra certainly put into action the philosophy expressed in that gem of Teresian wisdom. In doing so she had been converted by God's grace from a sour existence to a manner of behaving which proclaimed life is worth living, an expression beloved of the late Bishop Fulton Sheen.

I recalled Petra's experience some weeks later when a lady named Joan presented herself at the laying on of hands at 'Avila' following the prayer meeting there. Kay and I welcomed her and light-heartedly I said, 'In no way will we pray with you unless you smile'.

The poor lady stood transfixed for some seconds before responding incredulously, 'What did you say?'

I responded by repeating my observation as innocently as I could but sadly she mournfully shook her head, saying, 'Oh God! It's so long since I smiled, I really forget how to do so!' Joan looked so woebegone and grief-stricken I hadn't the heart or the time to pursue the matter further or to advocate in my best Clint Eastwood manner, 'Come on; smile and make our day!' Instead Kay and I embraced her, asked the Lord to console and comfort her, while praying that the peace, joy and tranquillity of the Holy Spirit should descend afresh on her. We never got to know Joan's circumstances or needs, nor did we strive to discover her problems. In 'Avila' we do not offer a counselling or advice service but we must have gone to the heart of the matter as Joan's tears became visible. When our two minute prayer effort finished she sincerely thanked us and then truly made our day by including, 'Now I'm going to try to smile!' In the film world, Joan's performance would hardly have merited an Oscar but it was a very moving moment for us, as we saw her doom and gloom expression fade as this strangely relaxed lady embraced us and graciously withdrew.

Understandably, the pattern of my life radically changed with the publication of my books on healing, quickly leading to press and radio interviews and TV appearances in Ireland

and in the UK, with the consequent stream of letter and telephone calls plus speaking engagements all bringing me into contact with various nationalities and cultures. I can therefore authoritatively state that the stories of Petra and Joan symbolise the world-wide presence of the enormous number of people affected by stress, people who, finding it difficult to cope, suddenly see their lives turn sour as worry consumes them. The knowledge that the affliction of worry is not confined to creed, colour, class or nationality has led to the view now universally accepted that those who fail to recognise, understand and manage worry have taken the first step towards the total destruction of the quality of life.

In this context then when invited to address Charismatic gatherings, 'How would you describe life without worry?', is a question I often pose. Believe me, the answers I receive are almost invariably, alarmingly negative, as demonstrated by the following examples:

'Life without worry is an impossibility!'
'Life without worry is a contradiction in terms!'
'Every mother has the privilege of worrying about her children!'
'I'm self-employed, therefore I have opted to live with worry!'
'Worry is the price of life so we only stop worrying when we die!'

This type of answer by excluding hope and even the possibility that there should be another way limits the whole concept of worry and those holding such views should realise before it is too late that this closed mind attitude could ruin their lives and those of their loved ones too. The hope expressed in time honoured phrases such as, 'The optimist always wins', and 'It is better to live in hope than die in despair', must be more attractive for human beings. Doom and gloom attitudes towards worry are surely sunk without trace by the homespun truths expressed in the logos, 'Today is the tomorrow you worried about yesterday', and, 'The future never comes'. Listen to the joyful hope expressed by another oldie, 'All our yesterdays are gone forever; nobody can bring them back. Conversely, no one can promise us tomorrow. All we have is this day. But worrying about the past and being fearful of the future destroys the only thing we are sure of – this day!'

Frankly, life without worry can be truly described as Heaven on earth. A Christian should constantly seek to taste this worry-free lifestyle, never forgetting the word Gospel is old English for Good News, a fact which makes me wonder exceedingly why the Holy Church persisted with a term that is unhelpful in the field of modern communications. How can Christians possibly hope to successfully announce the good news of personal eternal salvation while projecting personalities and appearances reflecting sadness and disaster? In season and out of season it must be stressed that it was the founder of Christianity Himself who unequivocally proclaimed, 'I have to set you free', a philosophy confirmed by the greatest interpreter of Christianity, St Paul, whose triumphant cry of hope, 'And be joyful!', contradicts and demolishes all evangelistic endeavour which does not constantly underline the kernel of the faith – the Resurrection and its glory.

Interestingly enough, I recall a wise gynaecologist, who, during the pregnancy of first-time mothers always warned them not to listen to old wives' tales. To hold and perpetuate then the false notion that motherhood and worry cannot be separated brings appalling distress to family life. A worried woman opts to present herself in the most unattractive manner possible with her mood as evident as if she were to parade publicly in a sandwich board proclaiming, 'Keep away form me! I'm bad news!' When a mother takes worry on board, her spouse and family sense a barrier immediately, leading them to shy away on the grounds that it is useless to try to confide in a wife and mother who obviously can't cope with her own problems. In this context, I well remember a lady approaching me after a prayer meeting and explaining, 'I'm frightfully worried but my husband and three children are unaware of it'.

'You must be joking!' I instantly responded. 'Why, from the moment I saw you, I knew it!' I need hardly add the realisation that her deepest secret was so plainly obvious to a total stranger was a severe shock to her. The Greeks had a word for it – 'The gods we adore write their names in their faces'.

Nothing in human life ever remains still; it either progresses or declines. Therefore when worry becomes the accepted norm in a person it will strive to contact a companion in the spirit of the popular soccer supporters song, 'You will never walk alone!' Worry never walks alone either; rather it will strive to introduce its active and ever willing evil partner – fear – that dreadful scourge of countless thousands world-wide. Unfortunately the arrival of fear is only the penultimate step in a journey to the black kingdom which seeks to invade the minds, spirits and souls of human beings everywhere with the saddest spectacle of all becoming apparent when worry and fear introduce their boss, the Boss of Bosses – depression. In no way do I make any apology for using this Mafia term as confronted with a person who has capitulated to worry, fear and depression is no different than meeting one whose life has been ruined by the action of an uncaring, corrupt, unreasoning terrorist.

When an eminent psychiatrist publicly asserts that if people could free themselves from one four-letter word – fear – he would be out of a job, it becomes plainly evident that people were never intended to live their lives constantly seeking help from counsellors and psychiatrists. Men and women should be well capable of coping without the need for 'uppers' and 'downers' to relax in the evening, with sleeping pills for bed-time. Should this practice become widespread, then generally speaking, it would demean and make a mockery of God's creation.

From this non-medical short study of the illnesses of the mind it becomes perfectly clear that the quality of human life tends to be destroyed should it be accepted that it is impossible to live without worry. In the Healing Ministry of the Holy Church it is abundantly clear that sickness is as wide as life itself, therefore those working in this ministry, endeavouring to bring healing to the sick by the power of the Holy Spirit, are constantly confronted by people seeking relief from the curse of worry. Now while nobody has the power to heal everybody, during the past decade and a half, I have personally witnessed worry vanishing from many, who by God's grace, have become involved in the Charismatic Renewal way of worship. This particular phenomenon of healing, experienced worldwide in renewal, apparently comes from the interaction of praise and the Word. Truly when people gather to praise God publicly, regularly, aloud, joyfully and unashamedly, they enter into and engage in one of the most mysteriously powerful disciplines known to the human race. While the praise of creatures certainly adds nothing to the glory of God as He is infinite, astonishingly one of its effects is the banishing of worry from a considerable number of those who participate in this group effort. Actually Renewal people rejoice in being known as people of praise. Seemingly, after a fifteen minute session of praise in words, songs of praise and tongues, the reading aloud of Scripture has an uplifting spiritual effect, utterly unique when it is sent forth in the knowledge and hope that quality, not quantity, is of paramount importance when seeking healing by the power of the Word of the Living God. To me it is one of the most satisfying sights in the world to see peoples' worried countenances change to reflect calmness and confidence during a prayer meeting.

Even a non-scholarly cursory examination of Scripture plainly demonstrates that believers of the Word are pointed resolutely away from the paths of worry and fear with this message loud and clear constantly spelled out in the Old Testament and Gospels, with the Acts of the Apostles through to the last book of the Bible, Revelations, repeatedly confirming this fundamental truth. As I have written previously, the words 'Fear not' appear 366 times in Scripture, a significant figure indeed, similar to the number of days in the year, plus one to provide even for Leap years. Likewise in the Gospels we read of Jesus Christ constantly advocating that those who would follow His way must turn resolutely away from worry and fear. In this context the following words of the Lord come to mind: 'Fear not little flock, for it has pleased the Father to give you the kingdom'; 'Let not your hearts be troubled;

believe in God and believe also in Me'; 'Why are you so fearful, oh you of little faith?'; 'I have come to set you free'; 'Come to me all you who are weary, who labour and are heavily burdened and I will refresh you. My yoke is easy and my burden is light'; 'Peace I leave. My own peace I give to you'.

Significantly we read in chapter 20 of St John's Gospel the beginning of the history of the infant Church, that following the Lord's ascension into Heaven, the Apostles and disciples with Mary the Mother of Jesus were gathered in a room, obviously terrified of the twin threat of the Jewish hierarchy and the absolute power of the Roman writ. However, we know from the Acts of the Apostles that when the Holy Spirit descended upon them in the form of tongues of fire and sat on the heads of each of them, instantly they went forth and joyfully announced the Good News of salvation. Their days of worry and fear were no more. Similarly people in Renewal are very much aware from the moment that the Holy Spirit descended on St Paul (then Saul) on the road to Damascus, for the rest of his life he worried about nothing and feared no one, only his Lord and Master, Jesus Christ.

On the one hand, despite the belief of Christians that their bodies are the temples of the Holy Spirit, it is a fact irrespective of one's sex or marital status, that every individual lives alone, a condition described by psychologists as the essential loneliness of personality. On the other hand however it is also universally accepted that worry, fear and depression are ongoing, potential, threats to the quality of life for all, Christian or otherwise. Therefore to keep these three destroyers at bay, people in the Charismatic Renewal movement look to the group power of the praising of God for the spiritual strength to do so. After all, the battle is not against human forces but against evil. In addition, people in Renewal strive to defend their emotions from attack or worry, fear and depression, by seeking to arrange time in their private lives, daily, to praise God and to pray. Finally, accepting Scripture is the foundation of the Charismatic Renewal movement, those in its prayer meetings rely on the power generated by the Word in these gatherings, reading it daily, to prevent them surrendering to self-pity.

Therefore they realise that worry, fear and depression are part and parcel of the kingdom of evil and are, as such, directly opposed to the Kingdom of God, a contradiction of the Good News.

Regretfully though, it is my experience that people who are overcome by worry and are overwhelmed by fear, are sadly quite unable to enter into the loud praising of God at Charismatic Renewal prayer meetings and lose both the will and ability to praise the Lord in their private lives also. Hand in hand with such rigidity, all attraction for Scripture vanishes from their lives too, while the laying on of hands and healing prayer seems to have no effect whatsoever on their condition either. Therefore I must conclude that when a person completes the dreadful triple progression from worry through fear and finally to depression, then the Charismatic Renewal way of healing, at its present level of development, is of very little benefit to these afflicted people. Actually one of the reasons which led me to write this book is the world-wide phenomenon of the widespread damage inflicted on people by depression, therefore it is of paramount importance that people everywhere should become aware of this alarming universal spectacle. In the never ceasing battle against depression then, the great blessing for those in the Charismatic Renewal prayer movement is the realisation that they have been introduced to a seven-fold way of worship which is of immense help in dispelling the two pronged attack of worry and fear. Should these be kept at bay by God's grace, then the spectre of depression recedes and one of life's glittering prizes, peace of mind, can be claimed.

Nonetheless, in this layman's review of the Charismatic Renewal way of coping with stress and strain, it is as well to remember that nobody has all the answers to the questions posed by life. The stark fact that we are mysterious people living in a mysterious world worshipping a mysterious God is aptly illustrated by the following true story which I rank as one of the most extraordinary experiences I have ever witnessed in my work in the Healing Ministry.

In one of my many journeys abroad a very dishevelled,

distraught-looking, heavily built, middle-aged lady approached me after a prayer meeting and straight away blurted out, 'I'm homicidal and suicidal!' As I stood, shocked, dead still and speechless before her, she expanded. 'With my alcoholic husband wreaking havoc in our home and as we are submerged by debt and disaster, it seems that the only way out for me and my four children is to kill him and then kill myself!' Not knowing what to do or say, in an automatic reaction, I reached out my hands to her but as soon as I touched her, it was as if she was snatched from my grasp and literally flung violently to the floor, the thud resounding round the hall! There she lay at my feet, face upwards, motionless, with eyes closed. Normally when people are slain in the Spirit or rest in the Spirit, they crumple in a very gentle way, but this lady went down as if struck by lightning! Not knowing what to do, I moved aside, standing close by to prevent anyone from stumbling over her and continued to minister to other people in a queue which had formed. Curiously enough, no other person in the hundreds present rested in the Spirit. After some ten minutes or so, the lady on the floor stirred and struggled to a sitting position so I bent down to assist her to stand up, but the instant I touched her she crumpled in a heap on the floor again!

Some ten seconds or so later, she came to for the second time, smiling and laughing as she warned, 'Please don't touch me, or I'll never get up'. I stood and watched in amazement as she sat up and now, conscious of her appearance, arranged her hair and tidied herself up generally, picked up her handbag and rose effortlessly, her face radiant. 'Oh thanks Andy!' she exclaimed. 'Thank you so much. It's all over. It's all over!' and confidently, with a spring in her step, she waved goodbye and left. What happened to her on the floor I'll never know, not in this life anyway, but I do know the pitifully helpless and hopeless female who stood before me initially left that hall transformed – truly a woman aglow. Certainly, as Christians have always acknowledged, the Lord works in mysterious ways.

Allowing for the Lord's mysterious ways, it must not be forgotten when Christians elect to walk through life in the power of the Spirit that they must expect to be constantly surrounded by pleasant surprises. Personally speaking, my first impression of religion, all kinds of religion, in my earliest years, was that it was a deeply dull and deeply gloomy affair. From this viewpoint, it also seemed logical to assume that while laughter might not be exactly sinful, it was certainly frowned upon, if not totally outlawed, in religion. Imagine my surprise then when I first came to Renewal to have it explained to me that my religion, Christianity, was not primarily a way of life immersed in doom and gloom, but rather joy, of all things, was one of the first fruits of the Spirit!

This new awareness was more of a culture shock than a surprise to me, so much so that I wondered why I had been sold so short by those who taught me my religion. In this frame of mind I was next led to engage in a do-it-yourself research into the nature and history of worry, so first I had a quick glance at the characters who were paraded by the Church as top Christians, otherwise known as saints and surprise followed surprise as this little exercise unfolded. I began at St Paul, remembering it is universally accepted as truly as Jesus Christ is the founder of Christianity, St Paul was its organiser. Here my surprises surfaced when I found Paul implored for the faithful to be joyful and to always rejoice. His life never reflected fear or worry or depression nor was he a prophet of doom; conversely it projected the joy and peace of the Spirit. In prison or out of it, in the midst of horrible persecution or when, with friends in peaceful surroundings, in days of success or failure, in times of vindication or betrayal, Paul was, I learned, followed by the saints down the centuries of time, as a random sample confirms, all adding to my surprise. For instance, St John Vianney reminded the faithful that while God commands His people to pray, He forbids them to worry, with St Ignatius Loyola the author of one of the best pieces of spiritual advice ever offered, 'Laugh and go strong!'

Surprise multiplied for me as I continued my investigation of how the saints of the Church perceived worry. St Francis of Assisi insisted that his brothers avoided appearing gloomy and actually classified those who worry as hypocrites!

Furthermore, he advocated that believers should always be joyous in the Lord, be carefree, amiable and gracious. St Teresa would have no truck whatsoever with worry either, displaying her outlook in another sparkling one-liner, 'From long faced saints, O Lord deliver me!' Note the use of the word 'deliver'; it conveys her horror of worry, any kind of worry, no matter on what it is based.

I also came to accept for a sheer down to earth no nonsense approach for those seeking how to marry Christianity to a happy lifestyle, she unhesitatingly gave to the faithful and to future generations this seven-fold fool-proof law of life. First, she advised Christians to never let anything worry them. Second, she asked Christians to let nothing dismay them. Third, she reminded people that all things pass. Fourth, she consolingly confirmed the belief of theists that God alone never changes. Fifth, she calmly announced that patience attains everything. Sixth, she gave startling news – those who have God lack nothing! Seventh, she concluded that only the possession of God satisfies all the needs of human beings.

But the icing on the cake for me was provided by a saint, to whom, God forgive me, I was never attracted, none other than St John of the Cross. I always associated him with the 'dark night of the soul' syndrome, and as I could never decide whether or not this phenomenon was a purely spiritual condition or a nervous disorder, or a mixture of both, I always shied away from his work. Imagine my shock then when I learned that he of all people maintained that those who love God swim in joy, are always on holiday and are ever in the mood for singing! Not alone was I shocked: I was stunned.

To sum up then, it is plainly evident that God speaking to His people in the Old Testament, Jesus Christ bringing the Good News in the New Testament, St Paul in the Acts of the Apostles and in his letters, the Fathers of the Church, psychologists or psychiatrists – no one has a good word to say of worry. In short, neither God nor man commends worry. Every human being born of woman has the gift of life, but sadly the art of living is achieved by relatively few, with the quality of life deflowered for many by the demon worry.

Basically, the theory I am advancing is that Christians of all age groups everywhere, irrespective of their circumstances can successfully keep worry at bay by constantly expressing and exercising their faith, thereby preventing the horrible progression from worry through fear to depression. Why, even when composing this chapter, the truth of this assertion was confirmed to me by the personal testimonies of two people in my weekly visitation to the sick.

The first of this pair was Mary, who, living alone, had just celebrated her eighty-third birthday. Sadly in a fall, she damaged her hip and had to be admitted to hospital. While the doctors had succeeded in repairing the injury it was found that her weight had dropped to a mere five stone. Consequently, Mary was detained in hospital where attempts were made to rectify this condition. She had been in hospital for some time when I met her and having only one visitor in the previous ten days, chatted away merrily to me. With her bubbly enthusiasm it was plainly obvious that neither her environment, age nor health problems had got her down, confiding how she had received a new lease of life on celebrating her birthday, realising she was rapidly approaching the end of her time on this earth. A fervent Catholic she calmly explained that she was looking forward to a new beginning and had no fear whatsoever of death. She was the youngest of eleven children, survived them all and was the only one who didn't emigrate, with her Dad spending the last dozen years of his life with her. During these years they formed a very special relationship, seemingly; now she was looking forward immensely to being reunited with him in Heaven.

The joy of this anticipated pleasure truly set her aglow. She was as bright as a button for her age as she outlined her conception of Heaven as a place or state of total renewal where she would be welcomed by the Lord, while enjoying the pleasure of the company of her extended family and friends, the vast majority of whom were there already, she affirmed. Continuing, Mary mused, 'How wonderful it will be never having to say goodbye again. After all, St Paul assures us that "in Heaven tears will be no more".' She went on, 'And if that was not enough, I'll remain in this blissful existence and fellowship with no need for either doctors, nurses or dieticians ever again, awaiting in a timeless eternal existence anticipating being reunited with my body restored to mint condition on the Last Day of general Judgement.' With her flow of words, it hadn't to be spelled out for me that Mary had earned her living as a teacher. Next, as cool as a breeze she smilingly observed, 'Isn't it a wonderful vision? And it's all true! So why should I be worried or fearful?' I assure you, it was the best homily on Heaven I have ever heard or am ever likely to hear. However, as I had another call to make and having spent almost half an hour in her company listening, unlike Mary's vision of the next life, I had eventually to say goodbye. She cheerily waved me away, saying, 'Thanks for the chat. Looking forward to seeing you next week.' But if I thought I was finished with celestial topics for the evening, I was very seriously mistaken. Astonishingly, more was to come. Much more.

Within minutes of leaving Mary I was sitting at Isabelle's bedside, this patient being paralysed from the waist down. She was 29 years old with an unemployed husband and a nine year-old boy. She had a yearning for years to go to Lourdes but could never afford to do so. Then out of the blue, Isabelle was put in touch with a Marian organisation who sponsor sick pilgrims not in a position to pay their way to the shrine and to her immense joy she was selected. A nurse from the hospital volunteered to accompany her too, making the proposition viable. Next, some weeks before departure date, a Social Worker from the hospital contacted my St Vincent de Paul conference based there, seeking funds to purchase clothes for Isabelle's journey, a request which was readily agreed.

Having returned from the shrine some days earlier, here I was listening to her as she breathlessly described her very first trip outside Ireland. In wonder and awe she told of her arrival at Dublin Airport, having coffee there and then boarding the aircraft, all pure magic. I will always remember her description of the flight when she said, 'Oh, Mr O'Neill, when I found myself flying I was so thrilled, I wished the plane would fly on and on and never land'. But land it did with Isabelle almost overwhelmed as she recalled the hotel, the shrine, the Masses, the candlelight processions, the crowds, the baths and the shops. I was listening to a fairy tale with a difference – it was all for real. The sheer delight in her countenance was a joy to behold, leading me to interject, 'The trip has certainly made you very happy. Obviously you would go again.' Isabelle's rejoinder was of the classic mould. 'If Heaven is anything like Lourdes, well, it must be a terrific spot.' At that moment it occurred to me that I was certainly having a Heavenly night!

Driving home from the hospital, I quickly reviewed the lives of these two patients. For sure, Mary and Isabelle could be classified as the least of the Lord's brethren, neither of them having affluence nor influence, good health nor rosy prospects. Both were marginalised by their age and illness respectively. But their Christian faith gave them a peace and a joy that one rarely encountered in today's world, with worry and fear far from their lifestyles. Mary and Isabelle also had positively, joyfully and unknowingly demonstrated to me the truth of the phrase beloved by the late Canon Sheehan, 'God's merciful dispensation'. Very roughly translated, it could mean that, 'nobody has everything and nobody has nothing', a philosophy scorned by the faithless. But whatever these two patients had, they certainly hadn't depression.

For Christians who are led to worship their Creator in the Charismatic Renewal manner the Holy Spirit has provided a fool proof escape route from worry. When I first came to Renewal I heard Scripture was the foundation of this prayer movement but as I never met anyone who endeavoured to extend or project this assertion, I was challenged to embark on my own research to test the validity of this claim. My first conclusion was very basic indeed and that was that nobody puts in a foundation and then walks away from it. A foundation is laid so that some structure resting on it will do so securely. As if reading from a plan my research next showed the ground floor of this structure was the praising of God. It couldn't be otherwise as it is impossible to read Scripture without discovering that all Creation is drawn to praise its Maker. At this stage (and I was only on the ground floor) I had to accept the praising of God is an unfathomable mystery. When theists praise God, it cannot add to His glory, but those who do so find themselves unexpectedly lifted up with their worries dispelled because they have turned away from personal problems to seek the face of the Lord. As I explored this structure further I realised that the stairway from praise led upwards to the first floor which very naturally consisted of prayer of petition. It had to be thus, as from Genesis to Revelation in Scripture we find God's people constantly making their petitions to Him, seeking relief from their worries and fears, their faith grounded in the belief that He is Lord of all and ultimately in total control of events.

Continuing my upward journey of research on the next and second floor of this supernatural edifice of Christian spiritual life, surprisingly I discovered the Healing Ministry of the Holy Church. Actually I never knew until I came to Charismatic Renewal that such a department existed, simply because nobody bothered to tell me! But there it was in Scripture in all its glory spread over the old testament and the Acts of the Apostles with almost one-third of each of the four Gospels devoted to descriptions of healing of all kinds performed by Jesus Christ and His followers who worked miracles in His name at His specific request. As a result those in Renewal appreciate that they are no longer helpless when worry looms. They expect to witness miracles and they do, with even my three books already published manifesting the awesome power of the Holy Spirit. Hopefully, this my fourth book, will do likewise.

As I persevered with my research, I ascended to the third floor of this structure where the presence and function of the Holy Spirit is revealed. There one can discover, again from Scripture, that Jesus Christ, after His death and resurrection, told His disciples that He was ascending to the Father who would send the Holy Spirit to them. Christ further explained that the Spirit would not speak of Himself but would only remind them of what Jesus said and taught. The forgotten third person of the Holy Trinity was thus startlingly brought into my understanding of Christian spirituality. Next I entered the fourth floor area where the first fruits of the Holy Spirit are freely on offer and among them, for starters, are joy and peace. From this elevated position, the pent house at the top of the escape route, it is easy to see the alternative way of life which begins innocently enough when people accept worry as one of the laws of life. But as worry is solely based on endless possibilities which might never happen, then it can have no solid foundation and can truly be described as basement living. Sadly in this basement is a trap door with leads to fear, an area where one is at grave risk of completing this downward spiral to the dreaded dungeon of the darkness of depression. Surely human beings were never intended to live in this condition which cannot give glory to God. I am quite satisfied that this is one of the scenarios which Jesus Christ had in mind when he gave His followers the last of the seven petitions in His very own prayer, the Lord's prayer. I am also satisfied that the good life is available to Christians on this earth through the upward thrust of the Charismatic Renewal seven-fold way of worship, with the unshakable Gospels, the pinnacle of the Scriptures as the corner stone of its foundation.

With two out of every three letters I receive from Ireland and abroad beginning with, 'I am very worried', and listening to these same four words in a similar ratio in local, trunk and overseas telephone calls, the universality of the affliction of worry is frighteningly demonstrated daily to me. In that context then, accepting the fickleness of human circumstances and the inherent instability of events plus the fact that nobody anywhere can predict when life will end, then one must conclude that Christians would be well-advised to use the Charismatic Renewal escape route from worry. Living close to, by, and in, the Word, praising the Lord daily, constantly petitioning the Creator for one's needs, seeking and expecting healing by the power of the Holy Spirit, while endeavouring to strive to enter into the joy of the Lord and so be at peace with oneself, with neighbours and with the Supreme Being, can only be achieved by daily application of this upward spiral discipline and of course, by God's grace. Thankfully His grace (or gift) is there for the asking, now that the human race has been redeemed by

Jesus Christ. Accepting also spirituality like every other aspect of human life can never be placed in neutral gear, failure to look upwards can only lead to the other route – downwards to eventual ultimate despair. Considerations like these lead me to set aside Wednesday of each week to concentrate on the things of the spirit with this mid-week day brilliantly ending in 'Avila', where I join hundreds of others of like mind seeking the Kingdom of God in a glorious festival of praise and the Word while surrounded by miracles. May it continue for many a long year.

Let's leave the last word on worry to Psalm 37 which warns believers in the One True God not to worry as only evil comes of it. Finally, considering the whole purpose of life for Christians is eternal salvation, which can be achieved by avoiding evil and doing good, then we will have to conclude that worry is part and parcel of evil. The true purpose of worry is to seek to deny Christians their rightful heritage – an unending existence in eternal happiness in Heaven, surrounded by God and those we loved on earth, when human life ends, as it surely will, for everyone.

3

HEAL THE SICK!

'Promises, promises, promises', is a taunt used when undertakings, although given with firm conviction, are not honoured. So conscious that we could not be tainted by such a reproach, I presume, accounted for the measure of job satisfaction shared by Val and I as we headed off from Dublin's Fair City early on a summer's Sunday morning in fulfilment of a pledge given months previously. Our destination was a small town in Ireland's mid-west region, a $1^1/2$ hour drive from our homes. There, several Charismatic Renewal prayer groups in the area had planned a day with the Lord and our function was to assist the organising committee to successfully complete their planned programme.

The morning session of the conference was of necessity flexible to cater for a farming community. Milking obligations and the care of livestock plus the fact that most of those attending lived considerable distances from the venue, resulted in people arriving in a constant stream up to lunch break. However, we managed to successfully 'ad lib' this period when I chaired a questions and answers programme, with the discussion centred on various aspects of Renewal. It was indeed very gratifying to note the general interest topics like tongues and prophecy aroused; obviously, men and women do not live by bread alone. This information session was liberally interspersed with the praising of God in the Renewal way with the Word also sent forth, all ensuring that the morning session of the conference sped as swiftly as on eagles' wings. Hopefully it was spiritually profitable too.

Hospitality at lunch was certainly lavish with the good people of rural Ireland providing an excellent meal for all. With the Word of God feeding the spirit and a table groaning under mouth-watering dishes, truly the best of both worlds was on offer in what was to prove a memorable Sabbath for those privileged to be present.

As it happened the parish hall where the morning session was held proved inadequate for the numbers who turned up for the afternoon assembly so the organisers were forced to switch the gathering to the parish church. Immediately the chairperson there called the meeting to order, a middle-aged lady sought permission to give testimony so one of the stewards took a 'roving mike' to her. She then calmly revealed that she was stone deaf in her left ear for years but at lunch was amazed to hear clearly the conversation and remarks of people seated to her left. The realisation initially threw her into utter confusion and it was quite a while before she closed off her right ear, the action confirming that the hearing in her left ear had been completely restored. Apparently it occurred so gradually and gently during the morning session that she was completely unaware of it, and now here she was endeavouring to come to terms with normal hearing in both ears. What a fantastic relief it was not to be compelled to swivel her head to pick up conversation on her left, she claimed. In her own words, it was a deliverance. She had also to come to terms with the medical prognosis that the hearing in her left ear had been irrevocably destroyed.

More confusion followed with the realisation that her deafness vanished without any specific laying on of hands ceremony of any kind whatsoever. However, it is now par for the course in Renewal circles that when God's people gather to praise His name, healing of all kinds tends to surface. This lady's spontaneous testimony naturally sent a ripple of excitement through the congregation who greeted the good news with loud and prolonged applause as the music ministry very sensitively led the gathering in the singing of 'He is Lord'. He certainly is, with the lady's story confirming once more that the Spirit blows where it will, when it wills. As one swallow does not make a summer, this healing was destined not to stand alone either.

The afternoon session was mainly devoted to the theme of

the Word, with the teaching outlining methods and examples of prayer based on the Word of the Living God, the most powerful form of prayer known to Christians. The conference ended with concelebrated Mass during which I gave a homily on healing. With the ending of the Eucharist, the whole gathering participated in this solemn ceremony of the laying on of hands with the four priests joining me in this simple but moving service, a tradition unbroken in the Church since Christ walked the earth, but revived generally in the Catholic Church with the coming of the Charismatic Renewal prayer movement. As far as I could ascertain, strangely there was no evidence of any healing visible when the ceremony concluded, but then one of the fundamental principles of this discipline is that the timing of healing is the Lord's alone. Significantly then, as Val and I were leaving the church, one of the stewards brought a lady to us, introduced her and she asked for healing. It was painfully obvious what her problem was when she extended her twisted and deformed hands, ravaged with arthritis, while exhorting us not to touch them. 'Should you do so,' she warned, 'it would cause such pain that I would either scream or faint!'

We stood with her and I asked the steward to join us in a very short prayer (by this time I was prayed out!) but he somehow seemed reluctant to become involved. Not wishing to exclude him and realising that he had worked hard and diligently all day at the conference, I asked him to place one hand on his friend. He still hesitated, so I took his hand and rested it on her shoulder. Next Val extended his hands in prayer towards the lady while I was drawn to hold my hands over her misshapen hands as it suddenly occurred to me that in the Acts of the Apostles, many were healed even when St Peter's shadow fell on them! It also became clear as daylight that irrespective of the person using the discipline of healing, the power comes from the Holy Spirit alone.

Meanwhile, the lady's eyes were riveted on her hands which she held palms upwards as we began to praise God. For some unknown reason then I let my hands hover very close to hers and was led to say, 'Madam, I am now going to brush your hands with mine, ever so gently. Should it cause you any pain, withdraw them instantly.' I did so. There was no reaction. Next, I rested my hand into hers in a handclasp as I enquired, 'Have you any pain?' But the lady was speechless, stood statuesque-like, all the while her eyes still glued to her hands. Suddenly she blurted out, 'My God! The pain is gone!' but simultaneously the steward withdrew his hand in very evident alarm, crying out, 'The pain has gone into my hand! It's moving up my arm to my shoulder!' As instantly as the pain hit him, it vanished, leaving him quite shocked. Meanwhile the lady at the centre of the action was conscious of no one as before our very eyes all deformity disappeared from her hands as she clenched and unclenched them, rubbing them together, amazed at the sight. People who knew her flocked round as she stared at her hands as if she had just discovered them. It was a sight I was witnessing in the Healing Ministry for at least the third time and believe me, it is forever new and thrilling. I think I thanked the Lord for His miracle of healing but the excitement was too intense to even attempt to organise further prayer of any kind. I'm confident though that the Good Lord understood that scene better than any of His creatures. After all He is more familiar with it, infinitely more so!

As the newly restored hands were the centre of attraction, I buttonholed the steward who had that very unique experience minutes previously. He had by then recovered his wits and freely admitted that although he was deeply involved in Renewal for years, he dismissed healing by the laying on of hands as child's play, something not to be taken seriously by a sensible man of the world. Actually, at this weekly prayer meeting when the ceremony of the laying on of hands began, he invariably baled out as he could not be bothered by such nonsense. He then went on to explain that he was requested by the lady with the arthritic hands to take her to Val and I, and having done as much, endeavoured to disentangle himself from the situation, only to be detained by me. Both of us were at a loss to understand the phenomenon of the sudden surge of pain which hit his hand and flashed like lightning up his arm before vanishing as suddenly as it struck, amazingly occurring at the instant the pain left the lady's hands. Thankfully he had no reaction, after-shock or fear as he laughingly remarked, 'Hadn't I a dramatic introduction to the Healing Ministry?' For sure, the mystery of the faith is ever present with the Lord's ways as far removed from human ways as the earth is from the stars.

As Val and I were about to leave the church and head for Dublin city, the secretary of the organising committee invited us to her home for tea. In this family setting we discussed the events of the day at table, with the variety of the food presented to us, reminding me of the cry of those with waistline problems, 'Everything I like is illegal, immoral or fattening!' At the meal was the family's nine year-old son who unfortunately had spent most of his life in hospital, so we also laid hands on him for healing at his parents' request.

Before we departed, however, a friend and neighbour of our hosts arrived with her eleven year-old daughter. It transpired that this little girl was a traffic accident victim six years previously, had suffered horrific injuries to her right leg and had spent considerable time in hospital undergoing numerous operations. The upshot of the whole affair resulted in her right leg being $1\frac{1}{2}$ inches shorter than the other one, her Mum explained, as she sought healing prayer. On the spur of the moment I knelt down at the chair before this beautiful child who was dressed in T-shirt and slacks while wearing clog-like boots with very substantial heels, the gear strictly in line with peer pressure. I lifted her legs off the floor, rested them in one hand and instantly noticed the heel of one boot only reached the end of the upper of the other. The sight looked so odd that instinctively I grasped the heel of the boot on the short leg and exerting a firm downward pull, to my amazement, saw the leg begin to descend! I kept the pressure on and down it came ever so slowly until the heels of both boots were perfectly level! I then withdrew my hand and the growing ceased. Meanwhile our host and the mother of the child, both dumbfounded and speechless, clung to each other, as I requested the girl to stand up. She did so. Next I directed her to walk round the room. She obliged and found that she had neither pain nor limp.

Naturally it took the two ladies some time before they recovered their voices, with our host exclaiming, 'Praise God! I've seen a miracle in my home today.'

Some months later, the little boy in the family with whom we prayed was once more taken ill and was admitted to hospital but died within days. One child restored to full health and hopefully to live out a long and happy existence; another taken to glory on the threshold of life. Why? No Christian has any remotely satisfactory answer to such a question. Although conscious of the age-old Christian observation, 'The Lord giveth. The Lord taketh away', it offers no reason whatsoever. Pie in the sky? Maybe so but at least it offers hope in the long run that on Judgement Day all will be revealed, a hope not open to the faithless who, when confronted by such provocatively puzzling events shrug their shoulders and say, 'It's the luck of the draw'. But by God's grace, Christians are not faithless; they live by faith. Christianity is a package deal presented on a 'take it or leave it' basis, where in many of life's tragically stressful situations the faithful must accept conclusions without any explanations. The alternative is to walk away from the mystery of their faith. But at least believers can always draw consolation from the virtue of hope, which binds love and faith together, the three theological virtues flowing from the Triune God, the very basis of Christianity.

ONE OF THE MOST impressive sights in modern hospitals is the range and complexity of the hi-tech gear available to the medical profession in the never-ending battle to heal the sick. Consequently in the huge multi-national organisations which manufacture and supply their equipment, Research and Development Departments are of the utmost importance, with their products constantly pushing out the frontiers of medical science, with new inventions now poised to supply hardware products for transplants. Even as I write, at least one patient is alive with the aid of an artificial heart, a development which is ushering medicine's 'spare parts' division into a new era. With metal joints replacements now commonplace, the age of the bionic man and woman may before very long turn at least one aspect of science fiction into fact.

In stark contrast to this mind-blowing computer based, incredibly complex, scientifically-led, appallingly expensive industry is the simplicity and awesome swiftness of healing by the laying on of hands which is part and parcel of Christianity, where the only cost involved is time. Even a cursory perusal of the healing of the sick in the Gospels shows Jesus Christ healing by a touch and a word. Amazingly at times He even healed by word only as demonstrated in the miracle of the changing of water to wine at the wedding at Cana in Galilee. Here there is no evidence at all of Him touching, blessing or even praying over the water. Similarly with the healing of the withered arm of a man in the synagogue on the Sabbath Day we read in the Gospels of St Matthew chapter 12, St Mark chapter 3, and St Luke chapter 6, that Jesus, who invariably spoke with authority, ordered the man to stand up and stretch out his hand. He did so but there was no record of the Lord doing or saying anything else, with all three Evangelists casually reporting that instantly the arm was better, as sound as his other one. In describing this particular miracle the three Gospels do not vary one iota but remain identical whether one reads the Revised Standard Version, the Jerusalem Bible, the New Jerusalem Bible or the Douay New Testament first published by the English College at Rheims in AD 1582, translated from the Latin Vulgate and compared with Hebrew, Greek and editions in other languages. The translations describe the healing as instantaneous, happening when the man with the withered arm at the centre of the action was obedient to His Word. The wonder of the Charismatic Renewal movement is that those privileged to be in its Healing Ministry (which of course is the Healing Ministry of the Holy Church) constantly witness the Gospels come alive in their lives, confirming the assertion one hears world-wide that the arrival of Charismatic Renewal announced the second Pentecost to Christians today.

The following stories certainly copper-fasten this claim and have more than a little relationship to events at Cana and in the synagogue where the withered hand was made whole.

A man named Alan rang me one Sunday evening in 1994.

In a no-nonsense voice he enquired, 'Are you a healing man?' and without waiting for a reply, he disclosed that he was crippled with back pain for months past, despite the best efforts of the medical profession. In no way could he even drive a car let alone continue his job as a driver of heavy earth-moving machinery. He pleaded for help. I responded as I normally do since I came into Renewal by pointing him to his nearest Charismatic Renewal prayer meeting and suggesting that he attend it weekly to praise God there for his healing, explaining that when people gather to do so publicly, aloud, regularly, joyfully and unashamedly, while sending forth the Word, healing of all kinds tends to follow. I added too that such a level of healing is not seen in any other activity of the Holy Church today either. Next, I recommended that he read daily for his healing from St John's Gospel, chapter 2, 'The Wedding at Cana in Galilee'. Finally, should this two-pronged approach be entirely new to him I mentioned my books on healing and considering his condition, specifically recommended my third book, where there is a section headed, 'New Backs for Old'.

Sadly, however, all I did seemingly was to totally confuse my caller, as he simply replied, 'Sir, I have no idea what you are talking about!' Apparently, I may as well have been speaking in a foreign language for all the sense I made! So, taking a deep breath, it was back to the drawing board, so, painstakingly I first endeavoured to explain as simply as possible what the Charismatic Renewal movement was, and how he might set about discovering a venue of this particular discipline convenient to his home, stressing that, 'by Hook or by Crooke' (as they say down Waterford way), he should get to it each week. Regarding the Bible, he disclosed, 'You know we have everything that twists and turns in our house but we haven't got a Bible!' I didn't waste much time on that problem, but told him to beg, borrow or buy one, emphasising it was so urgent it needed to be done yesterday! I was relieved when he laughed at that remark as it indicated at least that I was making some sense. To wrap up the instructions then, I added, 'Alan, when you are buying a Bible you can buy my book in the same shop!' You can take it that it was heavy going, but I stuck to my task and then, in the spirit of the Scriptural invocation of going the further mile, offered to pray on the telephone for the total healing of his back, should he consent. Reacting as quick as a blink, he blurted out, 'Oh, please sir, do. I'm in awful agony; I can't move without pain.' Straight away then I asked that by the sufferings Jesus endured in His sacred back at the scourging at the pillar, on Via Dolorosa, by the glory of His Resurrection and by the grace of the sacrament of matrimony his wife conferred on him on their wedding day, that he be delivered and resurrected from all back pain and from everything causing it. Finally I asked our Creator to be mindful that we were praising His name in the closing hours of the Sabbath Day, observed to honour and glorify Him and now hoped in return, that He would give us the healing we sought – there and then. I paused for a moment or two before being suddenly led to ask, 'How is the back now, Alan?'

His reply, I'll always remember: 'Good God, Andy, the pain is gone!' To say he sounded pleased would be the understatement of 1994 and as one can imagine he just went on and on, hardly conscious I was at the other end of the phone. Alan was simply thrilled at being delivered from the torture chamber of pain.

Exulting in the joy of the Lord in an automatic reaction, I punched the air with my fist like a soccer player on scoring a goal in a World Cup tie! As the man said, not alone did I enjoy the moment – I took pleasure in it! I also realised that after his stunning healing, Alan was in no position to continue normal conversation so I signed off saying, 'Congratulations Alan. Maybe you might give me a ring some time and let me know how you are doing'. Should he do so, I would then invite him to join me in praising God for His mercy in the spirit of St Paul's prayer in Ephesians chapter 3, verses 20–21. I returned to our sitting-room and resumed my reading of the Sunday papers, a clear case of switching from the Good News to the bad news, one could say!

As could be expected, Alan's wife, Mary, was also dumbfounded on seeing her husband so unexpectedly and dramatically delivered from his crippled state to full pain-free mobility as she listened to him excitedly endeavouring to recall his never-to-be-forgotten phone call to a total stranger. Her amazement deepened when she saw him hurriedly grab his jacket from the hall stand, put it on instantly and unaided, as he dashed to the front door calling, 'I'll be back in a jiffy; I'm going to call on my mother. I'll explain it all later.' Mary could hardly believe her eyes as she stood in their driveway, spellbound, and her husband, all six feet, four inches of him, strode athletically down the road as daylight began to fade on that early spring evening. Alan, like an arrow released from a bow was, apparently, rejoicing in and celebrating his newly found freedom of movement as he headed for his family home; he was certainly losing no time in fulfilling a solemn promise made on the phone moments previously. This whole scene was described in detail to me by a very interested third party, twenty-four hours later in an explosive phone call. Alan's ten minute walk was to have remarkable consequences too.

The very next day, with our evening meal over, I was preparing to leave home to visit the sick at St Vincent's Hospital, Dublin, an unbroken weekly custom now stretching back almost two decades, when my phone rang. The caller introduced himself as Brian, a younger brother of Alan. This man was certainly excited and it is to him that I am indebted for the information contained in the latter part of the previous paragraph. Brian, in full flight, now continued excitedly: 'Alan saw his doctor this morning, got the all clear to return to work, rang his employer and will be back in his job in the morning. He was so crippled, it's amazing to look at him now.' Brian then went on to describe how Alan burst into the family home and his widowed mother and his single brother were then treated to a display of PT exercises by Alan, I learned, as this man, almost completely immobilised for months past with a horribly painful back condition of unknown origin, demonstrated the power and the glory of a man in vulgar health. Alan then explained what happened during our phone call as his astounded Mum and brother listened. Next came a most unexpected twist in Brian's call when he revealed, 'You will hardly believe this, Mr O'Neill, but I'm a fitter by trade and am crucified with a bad back! Like my brother, the doctors are unable to help, I'm off work for the past month, and so here I am asking you to cure me !' Bad backs seemed to be a family failing, I accepted! As I hadn't much time to spare, I offered to pray for his healing immediately, should he consent. He did so willingly and readily. First, to put the record straight, I emphasised that I had no power to cure anyone; all I could do was to invoke the power of the Holy Spirit to heal. Next, I outlined to Brian the same three-fold recommendations that I gave his brother, and prayed with him in similar fashion. Actually, if my two telephone calls to this pair of brothers had been recorded and were played back, it wouldn't have surprised me if both proved identical.

When I finished, as Brian had listened in complete silence, giving no indication as to whether or not he understood my instructions, message or prayers, I finally advised, 'Should you be perplexed with my approach, do contact your brother Alan; he will explain matters and fill you in as to what you should do.' A quick glance at my watch warned me it was time to be on my way, so I wished him good luck, put the phone down, and made an act of confidence in God, trusting that the silence at the other of the phone did not indicate confusion, and headed for St Vincent's Hospital.

Returning home some three hours later, my wife Delia informed me that, 'A man named Brian called, and hearing that you were out, said he would phone again later this evening'. Delia added, 'He seemed to be very anxious to speak with you'. True to his word at 10 p.m., his appointed time, my phone rang; it was Brian, loud and clear. When I picked up the phone I was greeted with a veritable barrage of words which spilled forth. My recollection of his call was more or less as follows: 'Mr O'Neill, halfway through your prayers this evening, I had an experience of some kind or other. I couldn't define it; all I know is that I became very quiet and had no desire to speak. It seemed I was doing the right thing by just listening. Now here's the big news – when the phone call ended I straightened up and suddenly found the pain in my back had vanished! I couldn't believe it, I became confused but I walked into our living-room and shouted, "Ma, the pain is gone!" I needn't tell you she was shocked – and so was I,' he added. They weren't the only ones in shock – so was I on hearing his news! I continued to listen as in high glee he divulged how on finding himself cured, he too quit his home like his elder brother on the previous evening and walked to Alan's house to announce his deliverance! Concluding, Brian thanked me profusely but two instant healings by prayer on the telephone on successive evenings to a pair of brothers similarly afflicted left me so stunned that words failed me. On that same evening, hours previously when I finished praying with Brian he was unable to speak. Now it was my turn!

Later when I gathered my wits and reviewed these two happenings objectively I was amazed at the incredible lightning-like speed of cures which those in the Church's Healing Ministry are sometimes privileged to witness when the power of the Holy Spirit is displayed. I accepted too this awesome power is released when the Word of the Living God is sent forth. The promise of Yahweh unequivocally spelled out by one of the three authors of Isaiah in chapter 55, verses 10–11 is certainly not an empty form of words, that's for sure. Such a promise made to the Chosen People of God is not frozen either in a particular time-frame some 2,740 years ago; I had experienced that self-same promise fulfilled not once but twice on two successive evenings on the telephone in my own home. The realisation was mind-blowing.

People from 'far away places with strange sounding names' seeking healing tend to enter my life and exit from it in much the same way as actors do on stage. Therefore when I minister to people on the telephone, by letter or by personal contact, it is usually a once-off affair. Accepting this fact of life, I never anticipated that I would hear from or of Alan and Brian again, once their healing had been effected. But as truly as the Lord works in mysterious ways, the Healing Ministry of the Holy Church is subject to the same law, with events regularly and unexpectedly overtaking me. Some six months or so after these two dramatic telephone calls a lady called Elizabeth rang me in the autumn of 1994. She thanked me for taking her call, disclosed her name, address and telephone number and went on to explain that she was the mother of Alan and Brian. She also joyfully confirmed their healing while thanking God that both of them hadn't a moment's illness or physical inconvenience since their dramatic healing during prayer on the telephone in the spring. An independent witness testifying to and confirming these healings gladdened my heart as I hastened to give the glory to God for their cures in the spirit of St Paul's gloriously inspiring prayer in Ephesians, chapter 3, verses 20–21.

Elizabeth had problems with her right hand and forearm progressively weakening and, fearful that she might eventually lose the use of her whole arm, here she was seeking healing prayer, just as her sons did six months previously. As I invariably do I first of all pointed her to her nearest Charismatic Renewal prayer meeting, asking her to go to it and praise God there for her healing, and was gratified to learn that her sons had found one not too far distant from their village. With two drivers in the family I laughingly remarked that she now could have no more excuse for failing to attend these gatherings of God's people, praising His name each week! Next I stressed how essential Scripture is in the life of a Christian and recommended she read daily from St Matthew's Gospel chapter 12, verses 9–14, where the healing by Jesus Christ of a man with a withered arm is described. I reminded Elizabeth that in this passage of Scripture, we don't find Jesus touching the effected limb or even praying over it. The withered arm was instantly restored, happening when he obeyed the Word. As usual then, I rounded off my message with a short prayer asking her arm to be restored to normality by the power of the same Word which I had the privilege of sending forth and which she had received in faith. Elizabeth's call concluded when she informed me that she had a brand new copy of Scripture presented to her by her son Alan. In no way was he prepared to part with the family Bible that he borrowed following his spectacular deliverance, Elizabeth joyfully explained! In soccer jargon, I regret that I can't report a hat-trick of healings as Alan and Brian's mother did not receive an immediate cure as her sons did. However, I hope that she accepts that nobody has the power to heal everybody and that the timing of healing by the power of the Holy Spirit is the Lord's alone.

IN EXAMINING PRAYER OF petition objectively and dispassionately, one inescapable conclusion is that there is no particular type of prayer, novena, formula of words or pilgrimage to shrines anywhere available to Christians which can be guaranteed to bring success every time that it is used. The power of the Holy Spirit cannot be programmed, organised, manipulated, usurped, taken by violence or encompassed by anyone or in any place on earth. Consequently individuals who promote any type of worship or pattern of activity in prayer of petition under the banner headline, 'Never known to fail', do a grave disservice to Christianity in general and to people struggling to understand even in a limited way the philosophy of prayer of petition, in particular. Prayer of every kind is basically an attempt by a creature to contact the Creator, a non-material activity in which the whole person (i.e. will, mind, spirit and body) is engaged, and therefore it is, and remains largely, a mystery. The source of Christian faith is, as we know, two-fold – tradition and the Bible. Therefore when a prayer pattern or prayer style is based on the teaching of Jesus Christ Himself, it is founded on both tradition and the Scriptures, and as such is beyond criticism. One very clear example of this assertion is found in St Luke's Gospel chapter 11, verses 5–8 in the story of a man in urgent need of three loaves of bread. Here we also learn that the virtue of persistence is absolutely essential in prayer of petition if success is to be achieved. The truth of this assertion was splendidly confirmed for me in the autumn of 1994 when Delia and I were on a week's holiday in the west of Ireland. Leaving the dining-room of our hotel on the first evening of our stay, a fellow guest, Mary, approached, introduced herself and reminded me that we had met twelve months earlier in the south of Ireland! Although I had no recollection at all of that incident, Mary however, will never forget it after what happened following our meeting. This was her story.

Having read my books on healing and recognising me from my photo on the cover of these books, without hesitation she approached me in the rose garden of that hotel and disclosed that she had an ulcer on her leg which was diagnosed by her doctors as incurable. Her medical advisers appeared to be depressingly correct too in their prognosis as this ulcer remained open, sore, ugly looking and weeping for every year of twelve years. Mary also reminded me that shock registered on my face when she disclosed that she had faithfully attended an outpatients clinic every Tuesday morning for the past dozen years to have her ulcer professionally dressed. Moreover her doctors could not recommend any other medical centre anywhere in the world which might hold out the hope of a cure. Nevertheless despite the monumental odds against the possibility of a cure, Mary asked would I pray for her healing. She next described that I instantly reacted by touching her wedding ring, recommended that she attend a weekly Charismatic Renewal prayer meeting and suggested that she read Scripture daily before asking the Lord to heal her by the power of His Living Word 'Heal the sick'. Mary further recalled for me that the swiftness and directness of the whole encounter amazed her as the best that she had hoped for was that I might offer to remember her in prayer some time in the near future.

Now, here she was, one year later, on our second unexpected meeting, this time on the western seaboard of Ireland, about to reveal staggering news. It appears that on the first Tuesday following our prayer session in the rose garden of that hotel, on attending her clinic for the customary dressing, the nurse remarked, 'Mary, I'm almost afraid to say it, but your leg seems to be minimally improved'. The patient could hardly believe her ears but the surge of hope which swept through her on that morning, she will remember always. Then dramatically but quietly, she suggested that I look down at her left leg. When I did so, Mary observed that, 'You will see, Andy, that it is now without a bandage'. Apparently the improvement which the nurse detected continued week by week until some months later the ulcer had disappeared completely, leaving no mark whatsoever on the skin. Whether or not I was shocked when we first met, without a shadow of a doubt, I was shocked now; there she was beaming with joy as I gazed on the unblemished silk clad limb. Truly, seeing is believing. So, in another hotel, hundreds of miles from where we first met one year previously, I touched her wedding ring for the second time, but now in thanksgiving to the Lord for His merciful healing of her ulcer, giving the glory to Him. The ulcer, which the doctors avowed was beyond the present capability of medical science to heal, had vanished. It was consoling to realise also that when Mary recognised me from the photo on my books, despite receiving the 'thumbs down' signal from her medical advisers and in the knowledge that her ulcer had persisted to crucify her for twelve years, she still, without the slightest hesitation, sought the intervention of the Lord. Once more, it was a clear case of, 'Victory to the brave' for Mary, who refused point blank to be discouraged.

But life goes on, I was reminded, when Mary left me in a rush, explaining, 'Excuse me Andy, I must fly – *Coronation Street* is on TV in two minutes!' My last glimpse of her, as she made a bee-line for the lifts heading for her room to watch her beloved soap opera in the company of another female devotee, reminded me of the power and the glory of the Kingdom of God on earth and in Heaven, projected in St Paul's assertion in the first twelve words of Corinthians chapter 4, verse 21. It's worth looking up; it will repay one a thousand fold as it gives undreamed of hope to prayer of petition.

JOHN RANG HIS MOTHER-IN-LAW; his call was dramatic and telegrammatic. 'It's a girl! Mother and daughter are both doing well.' Joan had only time to offer congratulations when the message ended. She replaced the receiver, relaxed saying aloud, 'Thanks be to God', knowing how her daughter and her husband, who were proud parents of nine year-old twin boys, would now be experiencing boundless joy with the safe arrival of a little girl. Immediately she went in search of her husband and joyfully shared the glad tidings. Alas, that was eighteen years ago, but now she was a widow, living alone constantly having to cope without the comforting presence of a spouse with whom to share family joys and look to for support when sorrow came. For sure, sorrow had come to Joan on that very day by another phone call from her son-in-law, confirming her worst fears. Prompted by the maternal instinct, incomprehensible to the male species, Joan reviewed the intervening years in her grand-daughter's life since her birth. The memories came crowding in as she recalled how proud she and her husband were, standing at the baptismal font as the newest member of the extended family was admitted to the Church and rejoiced, hearing the name Maryann assigned to her. Images of joyful days came fitfully to Joan, birthday parties, Christmas presents and Maryann's first Holy Communion and Confirmation days. This introspective trip down memory lane was uncannily swift as a video played at 'fast forward' speed. Now following her son-in-law's phone call, another lonely journey through life's pain barrier loomed once more for Joan with the latest news of her darling grand-daughter.

Maryann had never encountered serious illness in her young life, being as hardy as the proverbial trout. She was very bright academically too and as expected, her school examination results qualified her comfortably for a place at university. Without hesitation, she opted for medicine, was accepted and hoped to achieve a long-held ambition to become a surgeon. Inexplicably, in late September, just weeks before she was due to enter college, Maryann fell ill suddenly. The energy seemed to drain from her, a condition accompanied by a frightening weight loss, resulting in the family GP hurriedly arranging her admission to hospital. Within days of her arrival there, Maryann found herself transferred to the neurology department. Naturally this rapid development in her illness left her family panic-stricken with deep foreboding as they awaited the results of the tests and investigations. Sadly, the verdict was that Maryann had not one but two brain tumours, both inoperable. Within minutes of Maryann's parents being informed of the diagnosis and prognosis, her Dad rang his mother-in-law, Joan, who, having heard the message sat statuesque-like beside her telephone for almost an hour. However, eventually Joan stood up, left the phone, changed her clothes, put on her make-up and drove to her daughter's home. There it was – all doom and gloom – with Maryann's Mum, Clair, crying incessantly while her husband John was mute with shock.

Joan was sufficiently knowledgeable from personal experience to know that in the presence of grief one should never even attempt to explain away the situation. Grief-stricken people's greatest need is fulfilled she knew, not by advice, logic or argument, but simply by family and friends just being physically present. As it was late in the afternoon, Joan took off her coat, rolled up her sleeves, put on an apron and began preparing the evening meal. Her two grandsons with their two wives would be arriving early in the evening for a family conference, so to avoid as much confusion as possible, Joan reasoned that it would be as well to get dinner over and done with, irrespective of whether or not any of them would be interested in food in the circumstances. With the meal ended, Maryann's twin brothers with their wives arrived almost simultaneously, all wide-eyed, tense and white-faced in shock. Dozens of questions were asked as Joan served tea but nobody had any answers so the family, using two cars, drove to the hospital. There it was confirmed that yet another medical conference would take place within days to decide what further action could be undertaken in the best interests of the patient.

The following afternoon Joan called to her daughter's home and found her drawn and red-eyed, but as they talked over tea and biscuits, John produced, of all things, three books. Quietly, she said, 'Clair, I'd like John and yourself to browse through these. Should you identify in any way with their subject matter, then maybe we could discuss it in relation to Maryann's situation.' At that precise moment, the phone rang, so Joan left her daughter, promised to keep in touch and drove home.

Late that same evening, before going to bed, Clair rang her Mum and described her very ill daughter's condition, although she had no further news from either doctors or consultants. As could be expected, the call wasn't of short duration. Before it ended however, Clair observed, 'Strangely Mum, when John arrived home from the office this afternoon, he glanced at the books you left here and seemed to be instantly interested. Actually, when he returned from the hospital this evening, he took all three books to bed with him.' Remarkably, not alone did John and Clair read the books, but Maryann's brothers also read them, all within five or six days, a fact which encouraged Joan to contact the 'Avila' Charismatic Renewal prayer group at the Carmelite monastery, Dublin. It was there that I first met Joan and learned the sad story of her grand-daughter's illness. Maryann had at that stage been discharged from hospital but returned every three weeks purely for monitoring purposes. Furthermore, Joan disclosed that my books had caused quite a buzz of excitement in the family, so much so that she hoped to bring the sick girl to 'Avila' as soon as possible, for healing by the laying on of hands, even though they lived a considerable distance form Dublin.

Some weeks later, in January 1993, Maryann, with her parents, brothers and grandmother did arrive at 'Avila', where two members of the prayer ministry with the Prior of 'Avila', Fr John, and another visiting priest, formally laid hands on the sick girl. During this short ceremony, rich in Christian tradition and wholly Scriptural, her family was also invited to lay their hands on her too and they did so with immense love.

Some time later Joan rang me; she certainly had a story to tell. On Maryann's visit to hospital immediately following her attendance at 'Avila', surprisingly her condition was such as to cause the medical team to detain her for some days, for tests and investigation. More surprisingly, although the result of this extremely detailed examination was not disclosed, the patient was still not discharged, the saga continuing when the parents were requested to attend at the hospital early one Monday morning, to hear the findings of the final medical conference. There, John and Clair endured awful agony of suspense for almost three stressful hours before their vigil was dramatically ended when a distinguished neuro-surgeon burst into their waiting-room carrying a sheaf of x-ray plates and print-outs. He looked absolutely stunned as he blurted out, 'Astonishingly, we can find no trace or tidings of any tumours in your daughter! In all my years in medicine, I've never seen such a phenomenon! We are all astounded!'

Instantly, John burst out crying, while his wife, so shocked she was unable to take in the wonderful news, cried out incredulously, 'Doctor, am I dreaming? Are you telling us our daughter's brain tumours have vanished? Did I hear you correctly?'

When the eminent medical man confirmed the good news, Clair and John simply clung to each other, endeavouring to come to terms with their daughter's deliverance.

Joan next described how the family celebrated Maryann's recovery with a festive dinner, rejoicing that her health was visibly improving daily. Naturally joy was unrestrained in that up-market restaurant but curiously Maryann seemed quite detached from the prevailing euphoria leading her Mum to observe, 'Darling, why are you so laid back on this wonderful night?'

Maryann, as cool as a cucumber, amazed the dinner party when she revealed, 'I can well understand you people being on cloud nine; after all you only heard the news twenty-four hours ago. Actually, I knew I was cured some weeks ago!'

Was she healed at the laying on of hands at 'Avila'? Did she sense it then, with womanly intuition? We will never know, not in this life anyway, but reviewing her whole story we find the four classical routes to healing easily identifiable. First, Maryann was a young woman on the threshold of life, therefore the will to get well, the recuperative power of mind, body and spirit was bound to be most powerfully present and working in her. Second, without question she was surrounded by family love at its deepest, a fundamental instrument of healing. Third, Maryann certainly had the benefit of medical skills at least equal to the very best in the world. Fourth, the power of the Holy Spirit was invoked for her and hearing it was on offer, Maryann opted to co-operate. Incidentally I never endeavour to tease asunder how or by which of these four routes to healing a person recovers; the bottom line for me is that a human being who was ill had been made whole again. I agreed wholeheartedly with the philosophy of the man born blind, who on being asked how this man Jesus Christ healed him simply replied, 'Whereas before I was blind; now I see'.

Another unexpected development flowed from Maryann's dramatic recovery and was told to me weeks later by Joan when she made yet another, 'long pilgrimage journey', as she termed it, from her home to 'Avila'. Mark and Damian, the brothers of the ex-patient, doing very well in the business world, moved in the fast lane of life, surrounded by those who dismissed all religion as a refuge for the inadequate and the fearful. Consequently when Maryann's illness was diagnosed as terminal these friends of her brothers had nothing to offer. Mark and Damian were now highly amused witnessing the culture shock suffered by their yuppie friends when confronted by Joan's startling performance. The spectacle of a little old lady neither bankrupt of ideas nor crippled with fear, stepping out in faith, motivated by belief in her God and love of her grand-daughter, thereby bringing off a healing against impossible odds, shattered the objective calm of this irreligious set. The clinical efficiency of intercessory prayer when made manifest in miracle, throws into utter confusion all who reject the existence of the spiritual. For sure, God is not mocked.

THE VARIETY AND UNEXPECTEDNESS of the circumstances which arise resulting in total strangers contacting each other to share an extremely stressful situation never fails to amaze me. Such an observation very definitely applied to my meeting with Veronica, a middle-aged widow who contacted me by letter in early spring 1993. Sadly, I then learned that her daughter Dawn, a mother of three young children, was a cancer victim who, having had a major operation some months previously, had recently been informed by her medical team that secondaries had appeared. Dawn and her whole extended family were understandably shattered by the bad news and although they lived 150 miles from Dublin, some friend of Veronica suggested that she contact me. In her letter Veronica freely admitted that she knew nothing of my background or activities, other than in some ways, I was interested in people in trouble. Now here she was, reaching out to me, enclosing a stamped addressed envelope in the hope that I could offer some assistance to her family in their hour of need. Responding, I wrote to Veronica, briefly explained my involvement in the Charismatic Renewal movement and my strange but consoling connection through it to the Healing Ministry of the Holy Church. Next, I pointed her and her clan to their nearest Charismatic Renewal prayer meeting, suggested that they read Psalm 91 daily, and mentioned my three books on healing, in the hope that this spiritually united family effort would result in the restoration of Dawn to good health. Finally I concluded my letter with a short Scripture based prayer for the total healing of this young woman.

Within weeks I received a phone call from Veronica, who introduced herself, thanked me sincerely for my kindness in replying to her letter, confirmed that she had contacted the Charismatic Renewal prayer group and was committed to attending its weekly prayer meeting. She disclosed too that she and her family were faithful to the daily reading of the Scripture that I suggested and mentioned that she had bought copies of my three books, reading them from cover to cover before passing them on to her family. Furthermore she revealed that neither she nor anyone belonging to her had ever heard of the Charismatic Renewal movement or the Healing Ministry of the Holy Church until she was put in touch with me. Meanwhile Dawn was having regular chemotherapy sessions which she dreaded, as she reacted very badly to them, appalled also by her extensive hair loss. Veronica concluded her phone call by asking for a share in the prayers of the 'Avila' prayer group that Dawn would receive the courage to persevere with the chemotherapy treatment, with her next appointment being just three days away.

Weeks later, accompanied by a friend, Veronica made the round trip of 300 miles from her home to 'Avila', having beforehand made overnight accommodation arrangements in Dublin. At the Wednesday evening meeting there she gave testimony that some days previously, Dawn tearfully left her three children in the loving care of their grandmother as she fearfully set out for her chemotherapy session, driven to hospital by a kind companion while Veronica expected to have the children for four or five days until her daughter had recovered sufficiently to be discharged.

Continuing, she explained that on this occasion when Dawn entered hospital, she was given the normal preliminary check by her medical team, but to her surprise was not immediately prepared to undergo her treatment. Strangely she was instead subjected to a day-long series of tests, x-rays and scans, plus an ultra-sound video type examination, all ending when the leader of her medical team informed the patient that her chemotherapy session had been cancelled as also had the normal three-weekly pattern of this treatment. Next, Dawn was bewildered to learn that as a result of their protracted in-depth investigation, no trace or tidings of any cancer was visible and she could hardly believe it when informed that she was being discharged there and then and would be contacted after an interval of six months. Dawn thanked her doctors, hurriedly dressed and rang her Mum with the good news. Dawn's husband, who was with his mother-in-law and his children, was so overcome with joy that he left his dinner untouched and immediately drove to the hospital to collect his wife, taking her home to her mother and children in triumph. Veronica concluded her testimony by disclosing that Dawn was visibly improving daily, her hair was beginning to grow rapidly while her GP was astonished at the reports forwarded to him by his patient's consultants which plainly stated that all the cancer secondaries had vanished.

Reviewing Dawn's story objectively, the one undeniable conclusion which arises is that from the time that she became unwell and sought medical assistance, all was doom and gloom until her family became involved in the Charismatic Renewal movement. From that moment, not alone was her constant bad news dramatically halted; rather it was reversed as she and her loved ones rejoiced at the healing which amazed them by its swiftness. Veronica freely acknowledges that the medical team certainly saved Dawn's life with their skills in performing the initial operation, but when secondaries arose, both patient and doctors entered a grey area, where prognosis was not even attempted. However, Veronica and the members of her Charismatic Renewal prayer group, being committed Christians, who step out in expectant faith in prayer, have no difficulty at all in accepting that the God whom they worship healed Dawn by His almighty infinite power. Come to think of it, it's not a bad definition of a miracle.

IT WAS A FRIDAY NIGHT in early January 1994, a very ordinary day indeed in my life. From daybreak the rain had pelted down piteously from the Heavens, accompanied by a howling wind. Delia and I drove to Mass in our parish church as usual, then on to the village of Blackrock to do the weekend supermarket shopping and returned home at midday. After lunch, I adjourned to my study and spent the afternoon slogging it out at my steam age typewriter, putting this book together. With our evening meal over, Delia left to play her beloved Bridge while I donned a pair of rubber gloves, cleared away the dishes and began the 'pot walloping' chore as I listened to the early evening news bulletin on RTE Radio. Sadly it was unrelieved doom and gloom comprising yet another horrible murder in Belfast, the awful war in Angola, the two armed robberies in the Republic of Ireland, black on black multiple murder in South Africa and horrible details of the woeful, seemingly unending blood letting in the Balkans as Croats, Muslims and Serbs continue slaughtering each other, side by side with their never ending peace negotiations.

So, midway through this horror story of a news bulletin, remembering the aphorism, 'The most vital control on a radio (or TV) is the knob that turns it off!' I did just that, in an endeavour to reclaim some peace of mind. Almost instantly my phone rang, so drying my rubber gloved hands I answered the call; it was to change my ordinary day to a most remarkable one. Picking up the receiver I was shocked to hear a woman's voice screaming down the phone! It would seem that switching off the radio had led me from the frying pan into the fire. It took me some moments before I could adjust to the unearthly din, until I realised it was a human being almost completely out of control. Whoever it was was howling, 'Mr O'Neill, Mr

O'Neill! You will have to heal me! If you don't, then within minutes of this call ending I'll be dead! I can't stand the pain in my eyes much longer!' Although these and similar sentences were punctuated by terrifying screams, I somehow discovered that her name was Ann, she was married with three children and was phoning from Northern Ireland. But more importantly, she was on the verge of suicide.

Ann screamingly told me the pain in her eyes was like daggers being driven into them, understandably preventing her from eating or sleeping for days past. The doctors, she claimed, had written her off and could only offer pain-killers and even these were now ineffective. The screaming with threats to self-destruct combined to make this call a truly never-to-be-forgotten experience, almost nullifying my ability to respond in any way. I attempted to explain that I had no power to heal anyone, but could only ask the Lord to do so. However Ann couldn't be listening, I accepted, as the screeching of this tormented soul continued non-stop. My poor attempt to pray seemed woefully inadequate but I persevered in the hope that someone in her home, a next door neighbour or even a passer-by maybe, might be alerted and come to her assistance. Without any explanation I switched from praising God in words to tongues in the hope that the strange sounds, meaningless to human intelligence, might distract my caller. Again I had no success, so as solemnly as I could in the circumstances, I sent forth the Word and then asked Our Heavenly Father in the name of His only begotten son Jesus Christ, by the power of the Holy Spirit, to take Ann's pain away. Next, I asked out of the blue, 'Is the pain gone, Ann?'

Instantly she bellowed, 'It's worse! Oh my God, nobody could be expected to suffer like this! I simply can't go on!'

Why, I don't know, but again I persisted by praising God in tongues as loudly as possible but the horrible noise seemed to go on and on.

Then suddenly, there was total silence. I held my phone remaining mute and motionless for some five to six seconds. It seemed a lifetime before I quietly, asked for the second time, 'Ann, is the pain gone?' There was no reply, so after a pause, I went on: 'Ann, my phone has not gone dead. Are you still there?' wondering had she collapsed.

'I'm now taking the bandages off,' a small voice whispered, apparently still terrified.

'Merciful hour,' I pondered, 'what am I into now?' but thankfully the roaring and shouting had ended.

Next, in wonder I heard, 'Oh God! Oh God! The pain is gone! The pain is gone!' as Ann repeated this over and over.

I was stunned into silence but in an effort to make some observation, I asked, 'Can you see now Ann?'

'Oh no! My eyes are shut tightly,' she responded, adding, 'but I'm terrified that the pain will return!'

Instantly I countered, 'listen Ann. Both of us experienced the power of the Holy Spirit tonight. Accept your healing and stop worrying about the future.' Finally, in an effort to console and encourage her I concluded, 'Ann, I wish you eight hours of dreamless sleep tonight, and may you welcome the Lord with the dawn in the morning, pain free with the eyesight of an eagle.'

Ann simply said, 'Thanks, Mr O'Neill', and our call ended.

On my walk back to the kitchen, believe me, at that moment, I would gladly have given my share of the Healing Ministry to anyone. However, life goes on and the pots and pans in the sink were my next priority.

Later in the evening I reviewed the whole happening, logically, as the thought came to me that Ann might have been living alone, single, childless, a person who had simply suffered a nervous breakdown, imagined the whole scene that she had described while confusing me with the Samaritan phone-in service. Again, maybe it was a hoax call, but Thank God, the Lord protects me from such attacks. Anyway if the call was a genuine or a 'con-job', the caller would certainly have qualified for an academy award for acting. Anyway as the permutations could be endless I finished all speculation, realising I might not become aware of the true story until I had crossed the Jordan! But as seems par for the course in my Healing Ministry work, events were to overtake me with lightning rapidity too, confirming the validity of this remarkable affair.

These began to unfold the very next evening, when Ann rang again amazingly composed and at peace. She thanked me for ministering for her twenty-four hours earlier, profusely apologised for subjecting me to the barrage of ear-splitting shrieks, but explained she was then on the point of losing control. Ann disclosed when the pain vanished so dramatically, she just could not come to terms with her healing; rather she was consumed with the fear that it was only a remission and would inevitably return. Her eyelids slowly opened apparently, she put her two younger children to bed, and rang her husband, who was in the UK on business, telling him the good news. However she could not bring herself to go to bed, fearing that when she would lie down and close her eyes, the awful pain would return. She eventually climbed into bed well after midnight, sat up wrapped in a blanket, rigid with sheer terror, expecting the worst, despite being in a zombie-like condition from lack of sleep. It must have been almost 3 a.m. she mused, when sleep overcame her.

Next, in wonder, I listened as Ann described waking at around 7 a.m., stunned at being totally pain free with perfect eyesight. Finally she asked for my address, wishing to confirm her healing in writing. We then thanked the Lord for his healing grace, knowing we were very close to Him, as all believers are, when returning thanks. This observation seemed to puzzle Ann somewhat, so lightheartedly, I advanced the view that the odds against people returning to the Lord to thank him for favours received were nine to one against, demonstrated by the reaction of Jesus Christ when only one came back to say thanks when ten lepers were healed. Consoled to know that both of us had the privilege of standing close to the leper who gladdened the Lord's heart when he returned, our phone-in prayer session ended.

Although it is universally agreed that bad news spreads six times, or more, faster than good news, in the Healing Ministry of the Holy Church expressed in the Charismatic Renewal movement, many general trends are constantly reversed by the power of the Holy Spirit. The truth of this assertion was again made manifest later that same evening when a lady rang from the UK. She introduced herself as Mary, gave her address and revealed that a friend rejoicing in the name of Sister Rita, had contacted her from Northern Ireland informing her of Ann's remarkable healing! Now here was Mary seriously ill herself, seeking healing prayer! Small world indeed, I realised, where even in the spiritual life nothing succeeds like success! Interestingly enough too when I had asked the Lord to heal this lady the thought came to me that I had been part of an international triangle of prayer linking Northern Ireland, the United Kingdom and the Republic of Ireland – a unique Saturday evening activity indeed, judged by any standards!

Ann's story was destined to run and run, I knew, when ten days later, her letter arrived and in the spirit of the incident, it did not lack surprises either. In it I read that she had already found her nearest Charismatic Renewal meeting as I had advised, attended it and even gave testimony to her healing there. For Ann, a very private person, it was a big step to speak in public, but she was convinced that the Lord wished her to do so, which was confirmed when the whole gathering of God's people there were deeply moved by her sharing. In her letter, Ann also explained that her condition was diagnosed as corneal ulcers and abrasions, her surgeon declaring, 'Nobody in medicine knows what causes or cures it'. I'm sure Ann had some startling news for that eminent medical person and for his professional colleagues too.

Christians down the ages have always acknowledged a walk with the Holy Spirit is filled with pleasant surprises. Therefore, in this context, it was most consoling when the following prophecy was received at the 'Avila' prayer meeting shortly after Ann's instant and magnificent healing: 'The Spirit is alive and active and most certainly inhabits the loud praising of God when His Word is sent forth.' Not alone was Ann's healing confirmed by three telephone calls within twenty-seven hours of her instant cure, and by a letter some ten days later, it was also apparently copper-fastened by a prophetic Word from the Holy Spirit spoken to God's people, gathered to praise his name while sending forth the Word in the Charismatic Renewal seven-fold way of worship.

A VERY EVIDENT FEATURE of modern life is the significant number of casual Catholics one meets, people who other than attending Sunday Mass infrequently, never give another thought to the faith of their fathers. In conversation with such people, their complete ignorance and total indifference to the Lord's commandment never ceases to amaze me. 'A new commandment I give to you, to love one another as I have loved you.' The obligation of a Christian to love one's neighbour is not a counsel of perfection or an optional extra; rather it mirrors the way Jesus Christ lived. Therefore, those who would follow Him must do likewise. At the very heart of the Christian faith is personal accountability, a principle flowing from the Scripture which plainly emphasises that it is appointed once for each person to die and after death comes judgement. While Christians believe that salvation comes primarily by God's grace through Jesus Christ, the mere possibility even of the Father asking one, on the day of particular judgement, 'Did you honour my Son's new commandment?' is indeed a very sobering thought. In no uncertain terms it helps to concentrate the mind on the ultimate bottom line for Christians – judgement.

In an effort to endeavour to honour the Lord's new commandment, for most of my adult life, I have combined with others of like mind in a world-wide voluntary organisation, the Society of St Vincent de Paul, whose basic philosophy requires its members to personally minister regularly and directly to people in need, irrespective of their race, creed or colour. While I have worked at all levels in this organisation, at the coal face in parish based work, through regional structures to national and international activities, for some years now I have attempted to give expression to my Christian obligations to my neighbour by visiting the sick in hospital.

This now familiar routine continued for me on a bright spring Monday evening in 1993 when I entered the hospital that I know so well and first headed for the chapel. There, I asked the Lord to bless the work I was about to commence while also reminding Him as I am wont to do, that I could well be elsewhere! With His infinite sense of humour, I'm sure He enjoys this observation too. Seriously though, I like making the point in my prayer that whilst I am not claiming to be better or holier than people engaged in innocent recreational pursuits, I am, at that moment at least, different. After all, I'm only following the instructions of Jesus Christ Himself who, when He was found in the Temple after a three day frantic search by His mother Mary and her spouse, Joseph (surely a puzzling and uncharacteristic action on His part), said, 'Did you not know I must be about my father's business?' So, for the next $2\frac{1}{2}$ hours then I did just that, by God's grace.

However, with the night's work completed, as I prepared to leave for the car park, one of my colleagues, Benny, buttonholed me and tersely said, 'Come on Andy! I want you for a two minute job'. Without more ado, he steered me down a corridor to a ward, explaining that he wished me to meet a patient whom he had visited earlier. This lady, Maura, mother of two school-going children, had a part-time morning job in a store. Sadly, she fell at work, seriously injuring her spine, left arm and left leg and had been hospitalised for some eight continuous months at various locations.

Although it was well past visiting time, her husband still sat at her bedside, as his wife was very distressed, being in extreme pain. Benny quickly introduced me, saying, 'This is the man that I mentioned to you; he lays hands on the sick.' Sensing Maura's pain was so severe that she was hardly conscious of who was with her and also, as time was not on our side, without advancing any explanation for my presence or seeking her permission, I instantly went into action. Placing my right hand on her shoulder, I softly enquired, 'Where is the pain?'

In reply, Maura moaned, 'Oh, it's my back; the pain is awful.'

So I moved my hand to her back, putting pressure on the pillows to avoid inflicting any pain.

'Oh, it's further down my back, near the base of my spine,' she whispered.

I slid my hand down and said, 'Lord Jesus, take this pain away'.

Then, after a delay of two seconds or so, I heard myself asking, 'Is the pain gone?'

Responding, Maura turned to me in wonder and answered, 'It is! It is!'

I gently withdrew my hand and immediately asked, 'Where is the pain in your arm?'

'Oh, it's in my whole arm from shoulder to hand,' she revealed, so instantly I made the sign of the cross on the arm, tracing it the entire length of the afflicted limb while I pleaded, 'Lord Jesus, please take away the pain in this arm now!' Again after a second or two I enquired, 'Is the pain gone?'

Incredulously, I heard her say, 'It's gone!' as her voice seemed to trail away.

Being acutely aware that it was now well past visiting time, with a glance at the door of the ward, I hurriedly placed my hand on the bed covers, where I assumed her left leg rested and queried, 'Is this leg painful too?' With eyes opened wide in some shock she confirmed it was very painful, so for the third time in under two minutes, I used the same formula, praying, 'Lord, please take away the pain in this leg, too, for Your glory'. Instantly Maura moved her leg, and anticipating my question exclaimed, 'The pain in my leg is gone! It's gone!'

Apologising for the unholy rush motivated by a desire to avoid the indignity of Benny and myself being ordered off the premises, in conclusion, I hastily enquired, 'Considering the Lord is so spectacularly healing you, have you any other problem?'

At this stage her astonished husband jumped to his feet and blurted out, 'Maura has a blinding pain in her head since Wednesday last and her doctor is to call shortly to prescribe a new drug in an effort to alleviate it.'

Reacting automatically, I placed my left hand on her forehead and prayed, 'Lord Jesus, by the pain You suffered in Your sacred head when You were crowned with thorns during Your Passion and by the power and the glory of Your Resurrection, please resurrect this lady from all pain in her head, not by my words Lord, but by Your power.' For the fourth and final time on this never to be forgotten evening then I enquired, 'Is the pain in your head gone?'

'Oh, it is! It is!' was her reply.

It was only then when I straightened up that I noticed Benny had his hands on the patient's feet, right through the healing, so I said, 'Come on, Benny. Let's thank the Lord and get out of here before we are thrown out!' In keeping then with the 100 mile an hour pace of the encounter, we made our farewells, leaving a pain free patient gazing at us in wonder with her husband standing rigidly beside her, speechless, and headed for the exit. I can't recall our conversation as we walked to our cars, but Benny's face was certainly aglow.

As far as I was concerned, that was the end of the matter, but Benny reacted positively by calling at the hospital the following evening. He went to the ward where we visited Maura but she wasn't there. Instantly he chased around to the nurses station where he was informed that Maura had been discharged that afternoon.

In retrospect, as I had never experienced four distinctly separate instant healings and in such swift succession too, Maura's story broke new ground for me in the Healing Ministry. Also I would be less than honest if I didn't admit how I would have loved to be a fly on the wall of her ward when the doctor arrived later on that momentous Monday evening to find his healing skills were no longer required. Similarly I would have been intensely interested to have heard the observations of Maura's medical team the following Tuesday after their examination of the patient which resulted in her discharge from hospital. The one stark fact in this true tale which cannot be denied is that between the last time Maura was checked by the medical staff on the Monday and the arrival of the doctor late on that same evening, two men unexpectedly visited her, laid their hands on her in the name of the Lord, and witnessed a miracle. To attempt to use any word other than miracle to describe the instant, dramatic and complete change in Maura's physical condition after the laying on of hands, would be utterly inaccurate, patently unscientific or at worst downright dishonest.

Finally for the benefit of fringe Christians and non-practising Catholics who project the 'couldn't care less' or 'to hell with it' attitude to the faith and who may have forgotten what the Lord's new commandment implies, it would be in their very best interests to embark on a refresher course without delay. After all, the most important, undeniable fact of life is that the first of the four last things will inevitably happen, i.e., death, judgement, Heaven and Hell. Hopefully then, by Christian faith, God's grace and the power of the Lord Jesus Christ, practising Christians will have a happy transfer at terminal death to eternal life, a successful particular judgement and so avoid the fourth of these last things, in whatever shape, place, state or condition it exists. For me, that is a very important motivator.

4

CHRISTIAN LIFE

Dick, a friend of mine, was highly amused to learn of my interest and work in the Healing Ministry of the Holy Church, maintaining that as it is impossible to discover the Will of God in illness, it is therefore illogical to pray for healing. He had, in my view, an utterly simplistic approach to the problem, holding as it might be God's will that a sick person should not recover, how then could one ever pray for healing? Although a practising Catholic, prayer of petition did not form any significant part of his prayer life, apparently. Dick, an honours student right through his academic life, majoring in mathematics and languages, attracted to these disciplines by the rigid sense of order beloved of mathematicians and grammarians, could not come to terms with prayer of petition, deeming it an inexact science. Responding, one could argue that in many instances medicine too is an inexact science but no one in their right mind could advance the theory that therefore medicine should not be practised. However, let's not confuse the issue, but return to face head on, Dick's difficulty, applying ourselves to ascertain whether or not it is possible to discover the will of God in a particular situation, or maybe, more importantly, in our own lives.

The will of God is at the very heart of Christianity. We know this as the first recorded words of Jesus Christ in the Gospels are found in chapter 2 of St Luke's Gospel, where, at twelve years of age, He asked His mother, 'Why were you looking for Me? Did you not know that I must be about My Father's business?' Furthermore, we know His last words at death were, 'Father, into Your hands, I commend My Spirit'. Therefore we can be certain that Jesus Christ came from the Father, to do the Will of the Father, and having done so, returned to the Father. Actually, we can truly say that the public life of Jesus Christ on earth lies between his first and last words. Maybe then, before examining the prayer of petition, we should first explore a method, as Christians, of discovering the Will of God in our own lives.

No one can dispute that one can be certain of being in God's Will primarily by accepting that the ten commandments laying down guide lines for behaviour right through life while acknowledging too that all of these must be taken on board without exception. Despite all the information available presently by high tech press button hardware, it might be more than interesting to list these absolute terms of reference for Christians:

> First, I am the Lord your God; you shall not have strange gods before me.
> Second, you shall not take the name of the Lord your God in vain.
> Third, remember you keep holy the Sabbath day.
> Fourth, honour your father and your mother.
> Fifth, you shall not kill.
> Sixth, you shall not commit adultery.
> Seventh, you shall not steal.
> Eighth, you shall not bear false witness against your neighbour.
> Ninth, you shall not covet your neighbour's wife.
> Tenth, you shall not covet your neighbour's goods.

I know too (because I was taught and remember) that the first three commandments govern a believers relationship with the Creator with the next seven regulating conduct towards the neighbour. I am also aware that times change, a fact of life made starkly plain to me recently when a 20 year-old Catholic student casually observed that she had no idea whatsoever of the commandments. She also advanced the view that none of her female friends would know them either, although all had received convent educations. The rights and wrongs of social issues, debated in the classroom, was her only memory of Religious Education classes! It is important to realise too that as our conversation was on a one to one basis over coffee on a social occasion, there was no peer pressure factor operating. When I endeavoured to move the conversation along by enquiring whether or not she had any recollection of the seven deadly sins, she ceased taking me seriously and abruptly revealed that none of her set, neither boy nor girls, were even remotely interested in such topics! I was then left alone with my coffee, acknowledging once more that interest is the basis of memory. So, for those who believe (are there that many around nowadays, I often wonder?) the ten commandments are there; these won't go away and believers cannot adopt an 'a la carte' attitude towards them.

The starting point then in discovering the Will of God must lie in the acceptance and observation of these ten laws of life with the second step coming with the realisation that the seven deadly sins of pride, covetousness, lust, anger, gluttony, envy and sloth must also be avoided in their entirety, forming another non-negotiable package deal for Christians. Next in line comes the absolute necessity of fulfilling the duties of one's state of life to the best of one's ability, a challenge which begins when one comes to the use of reason and lasts until death. The fourth signpost on this search indicates the obligation of loving one's neighbour, copper-fastened by Christ's own words, 'A new commandment I give to you, to love one another as I have loved you'. There are no exceptions, reservations or 'special circumstance' clauses in this edict either with the oft quoted, 'Surely I can love some people and not like them' being a cop out. There is no substitute for love. The fifth and final hurdle to be negotiated is that Christians must come to terms with prayer on two levels – in their public and private lives. It must be so, as one of the most striking characteristics of Jesus Christ is that He was a person of prayer. Therefore those who would follow Him must also be prayerful people. This *via quinguae* (with apologies to St Thomas Aquinas!) five-way method is possibly the nearest Christians can come to discovering God's Will in their lives. Whatever else may be said of it, all five steps reflect traditional fundamental Christian principles while being totally Scripturally based. Nevertheless, religion being a personal one-to-one relationship with the

Creator, the final arbiter in knowing God's Will must be one's conscience. Surely any decision taken in conscience in the light of the five-way method outlined must be classified as fully informed, valid and wholly in keeping with the dignity of a human being, created with free will.

Having come thus far we now proceed to examine how the Will of God affects prayer of petition and here we first look to Scripture for direction. In the divine and living Word of God we meet generations of Jewish people in the Old Testament, living out their lives praising God and petitioning Him constantly for their needs, as Christianity has its roots in Judaism. This tradition was faithfully adhered to by Jesus Christ. We read in the Gospels that when His disciples asked to be taught to pray, He gave them a form of words universally known as the Lord's prayer, wherein He begins by acknowledging the existence of His Father (and theirs) in heaven while praising His name, all by way of an introduction to seven petitions. He then instructs His followers first to intercede that His father's Kingdom should come into existence, banishing forever worldly rule and the kingdom of evil, before requesting them to pray that the Father's will be done on earth as perfectly and completely as it is observed in Heaven. His next five petitions are positive, clear and universally addressed to all people in every age. In these petitions, Jesus Christ teaches His flock to ask the Father to grant the food needed daily to sustain life, to seek forgiveness of their sins, reminds His faithful of the need to forgive those who offend them, to plead that they should not be tempted to transgress His way and finally to seek deliverance from evil. It is very noticeable that Jesus Christ did not qualify in any way the last five petitions of His prayer to the Father by adding, 'If it is in accordance with Your will'. On the contrary, having first acknowledged the existence of that Will and alerting and making His people aware of it, He then proceeds to instruct them to ask positively, simply and confidently for their needs, without any exceptions or reservations. Therefore when I hear anyone ending a prayer of petition with the words, 'but may Your will be done', I wonder is such an addition a way of 'hedging one's bets'? For sure, this type of addendum is certainly not in the spirit of the Lord's prayer.

At this stage it is as well to remind ourselves of the primacy of the Lord's prayer. Sadly in my school days, nuns, brothers and priests (in that order!) who taught me my Christian religion, very definitely appeared to downgrade it and gave the impression that prayers associated with novenas, saints and shrines both at home and abroad were more important. This impression was conveyed when all such prayers invariably ended with the faithful instructed to add three Our Fathers, three Hail Marys and one Gloria to the prayer of the particular saint being promoted. Imagine my surprise when coming to the Charismatic Renewal experience, I realised how wrong this approach was. Now I know no prayer was, is or ever will be, more powerful or more spirit-filled than the Lord's prayer. By its very nature it takes precedence over all prayers composed by any man or woman, canonised or not, for the Lord's prayer was given to the disciples by Christ Himself and faithfully handed on from generation to generation to our time. It is part of the Word and is honoured by the Holy Church by its inclusion in the Eucharist, the primary, and most necessary act of worship for Catholics everywhere. 'It is the Mass that matters.' No prayer other than the Word is allowed into Mass.

Actually, Mass is, among other things, a celebration of the Word. In the first part of Mass the faithful hear and are encouraged to join with the priest in the readings from Scripture before standing to honour the Word from the Gospels. The second part of the Mass concentrates on the breaking of the bread and the blessing of the wine with the words of consecration wholly and totally Scriptural. It is on these solid and traditional grounds, confirmed by the teaching of the Church and based on Scripture, that I hold that the Lord's prayer has been given to Christians by One who is true God and true Man, the second person of the triune God, the One who has redeemed the human race. How beautiful and consoling it is to read too in the encyclical, *The Redemptive Mission of the Church*, by Pope John Paul II, that nothing can be parallel to or even complementary to the Word. Possibly the impression I formed that the

Lord's prayer was one to be added after the recitation of other prayers composed by people, was due to those who passed on the Christian religion (God bless them) to my generation and who were not Scriptural people. Therefore what they had not got they could not give and that was their loss and mine. But I rejoice to realise that one of the great graces (i.e. gifts) of involvement in Charismatic Renewal is that it opens the Scripture to the people of God with the Holy Spirit, recalling that the first definitive action of the Risen Christ happened on Resurrection Day, when he opened the Scriptures to two disciples on the road to Emmaus. It is on record that their hearts burned within them when he did so, a prelude to that tremendous moment when Cleopas and his companion recognised Him in the breaking of the bread.

Should my friend Dick ever read this particular passage of my book, surely he will come to understand that the Founder of the faith he practises, wished His followers to ask the Father in His name, for all their needs. It is part of the Christian way of life and in no way can the Will of God be an obstacle to it.

For many years now, as a result of my exposure to the Charismatic Renewal prayer movement, I do everything in the power of the Holy Spirit. Likewise, every time that I leave home I go forth in the power of the same Spirit. Why not? The Lord is only a prayer away and it was Jesus Christ Himself who stressed that the Kingdom of God is within believers, a fundamental principle of the Christian faith which must have inspired St Paul's prayer in his first letter to the Corinthians chapter 5, verse 20. So, having set out on a west of Ireland holiday in the power of the Holy Spirit, I had very quickly witnessed, on learning from the lady in our hotel, the slow but irresistible healing of a condition deemed incurable – the disappearance of the ulcer on her leg which began from the moment His awesome power was invoked.

GIVEN THAT THE HOLY Spirit is working in groups outside the Church, in movements in which the Church has no input whatsoever, what message is that proposition sending to the Church? Could it be that the 'institutional' or 'structured'

the other familiar disciplines. Possibly the introduction of optional celibacy would attract more applicants to the priestly state too, and even eventually the feasibility of the ordination of women must be addressed. After all, women form 50% of the human race and the Catholic Church too. The disappearance of seminaries, trainee priests at universities, the ordination of women – these controversial subjects, love them or leave them, won't go away. Although married lay deacons are now being ordained widely, this development does not effectively meet the basic need of supplying much needed priests.

An essential part of the dream of a new Church structure concerns the system in operation where priests and parish priests are appointed to parishes without any consultation with, or references to, parishioners. Such a procedure at first glance can hardly promote the bonding of priests and people into an effective unit. Could there possibly be another way? Let's dream on! Suppose there was an efficient Church structure as outlined above, in an unbroken line of communication from the family unit to Rome itself, then surely at diocesan level arrangements could be made whereby a bishop and his board of advisers would meet with parish representatives and discuss the appointment of a priest and a pastor to a parish. Presently, priests and pastors arrive and are transferred without any consultation whatsoever with the flock. At best, this system separates clergy and laity, it promotes a 'them' and 'us' atmosphere and in no way can it assist in projecting an image of solidarity, nor help in any way to achieve it either. Another thing; could this new association of priest and people, as outlined, operate and become effective at every level of our Church of the future? The present closed system whereby clerical appointments are made can hardly be maintained in this age where openness, accountability and transparency is demanded and is the norm everywhere. Come to think of it, the present Church organisation and structure when viewed in relation to evangelisation (which is the bottom line for the existence of the Church, anyway) cannot be defended when one realises the little impact it has made on the world's population – 2,000 years of effort! There must be a better way! Frankly, I'm often envious when I read of our separated brethren and realise that clergy and laity, both male and female, sit together at conferences with equal responsibility and status, all involved in decision-making at every level in their various Churches. Could a similar type of organisation operate successfully in the Catholic Church of the future and lead to a priestly celibacy being optional, be instrumental in women priests becoming a fact of life and be responsible for the laity having a say in all clerical appointments in the whole Church? Far fetched? Not really when one accepts that without exception, everything changes in this world of ours. Nothing remains the same and constant except the triune God. Change at every level of the Church should not threaten a Christian either, as Jesus Christ Himself said He would be with His Church until the end of time. Interestingly too He never said it would not change in structural organisation or have a set of rules which would be unalterable. More importantly however, real lay participation in the Church would at least ensure that the possibility of people being manipulated would become extremely remote.

Maybe our Church needs many senior citizens who dare to dream dreams, with those on the threshold of life not fearful to accept startlingly exciting visions, all inspired by the Holy Spirit, so that clergy and laity may 'go for it' together to achieve what prophets of doom consider impossible goals. Anyway, dreamers and visionaries always preceded great events, and long before Martin Luther King's time too. But don't take my word for it; look it up for yourself, in the Acts of the Apostles chapter 2, verses 17–21 and you will find it was advocated by no less a person than the first Pope within minutes of the birth of the Church. St Peter no more than myself wasn't expressing a new idea either as he was quoting from the prophet Joel who walked the earth 400 years before Peter. It was Joel's prophecy in chapter 3, verses 1–5 in his book in the Old Testament that was outlined to the amazed crowds in Jerusalem at nine o'clock in the morning on the First Pentecost Day. Is it any wonder then that the Charismatic Renewal prayer movement is often referred to as the Second Pentecost, when one man (Andy O'Neill!) under its influence, dares to dream of an entirely new Church structure? Truly, as the man said, there is nothing new under the sun.

IN 'AVILA', ANN ARRIVED in the prayer ministry room after the Wednesday evening gathering on the week before the Euro elections, in the Republic of Ireland. The queue was so long that the prayer team was compelled to work on a one to one basis rather than in pairs, so Ann was directed by the stewards to Tess. It transpired Ann suffered from chronic insomnia and in her own words, 'hadn't slept for years', despite the best efforts of those in the caring professions. Tess prayed that a normal sleep pattern might be restored to Ann, and, having spent three or four minutes doing so, Ann thanked her newly found friend for ministering to her and retired leaving Tess free to attend to the next person in line. Two weeks later a friend of Ann's conveyed the good news to Tess – Ann was healed of her insomnia almost instantly and was rejoicing, having received the gift of six to eight hours of dreamless sleep nightly.

I was discussing this remarkable healing of insomnia by the power of the Holy Spirit with a man who regularly attends the 'Avila' prayer meeting, our chat taking place only days after the results of the MEPs elections were announced. With a mischievous grin my friend observed, 'We have just seen three out of the four European Parliament seats allotted to Dublin filled by women and now you tell me of a lady in the prayer ministry in "Avila" who has the gift of healing'. He added, 'I wonder is this Women's Liberation movement going into overdrive to steamroll the mere male!' His good-humoured banter reminded me of the first time that I witnessed female altar servers in action, the sight moving me to visit the sacristy after that particular Mass. There, I was confronted by the sacristan, a woman no less, and when I expressed my sheer delight at this completely new spectacle for me, she replied with a twinkle in her eye, 'Yes indeed, our serviettes are so precious to us!' This description of altar servers 'made my day', as the man said.

How much longer before optional celibacy in the Catholic

priesthood will be the norm, maybe to be followed by the ordination of married men! Impossible? 'With God, nothing is impossible', is the core belief and while it is a fact of life that nothing remains static anywhere on this earth, we must accept that the widespread changes in the practices and customs of the Catholic Church over the last 40 years are so numerous that to attempt to comprehensively list them would be quite beyond my capabilities. But let us recall just a few of the things which were once regarded by the Catholic Church as sinful:

> i) *eating meat on Fridays*
> ii) *attendance at any service whatsoever of our separated brethren*
> iii) *eating more than one full meal on any weekday during Lent*
> iv) *receiving Holy Communion at morning Mass without having fasted from midnight the previous day.*

All these rules and regulations have now sunk without trace and when we look at them objectively we see them as an imposed pattern of behaviour which people nowadays find almost impossible to visualise. Actions considered sinful in the past by the Church are now not sinful at all. Could it be that the magisterium of the Church changes when the faithful vote with their feet? It is a consideration which must lend credence to the widely held view that that Church never does anything until it has to! However, since Vatican II, by the power of the Holy Spirit apparently, the Church has put the emphasis in many areas on the affirmative, proclaiming first the Good News while at the same time being conscious of the sinfulness of all. Change everywhere is unstoppable so it is only rational to be open to it, in the knowledge that whatever shape the Catholic Church may take in the future, every Catholic has the comfort, consolation and the absolute guarantee from none other than Jesus Christ Himself, who so reassuringly promised He will be with His Church until the end of time, come hell or high water. For me, that is the bottom line in any discussion on future trends in the Church. It is ultimately in the hands of the One Who is infinitely more capable than any Women's

Liberation Movement, Liberation Theology developments or the combined efforts of the right and left wings in the Church. So why not sit back and enjoy the ever-changing colours of life in the Church? After all, it was Jesus Christ who said, 'Let not your hearts be troubled'.

I have always maintained that involvement in Renewal has, more than anything else in life, released me in joy. Hopefully it is the joy of the Lord, one of the first fruits of the Spirit. In pre-Renewal times, although I at least knew that it was not a sin to laugh, I just couldn't see how a light-hearted and cheerful approach to the spiritual life could co-exist with my Catholic tradition and teaching. I am now convinced that my difficulty primarily arose from the absence of Scripture in my life, as those who passed my religion and tradition on to me, God bless them, were not Scriptural people. With the coming of Renewal I am now 'into' Scripture and have some understanding of its place in the Christian life and in my Church. Also, the more I dip into the Gospels, Acts of the Apostles, the Letters of St Paul and the others, the more I appreciate that this discipline promotes hope and joy. Consequently I now accept that there is much more truth than fiction in the old adage, 'Laughter is the best medicine', provided that one does not laugh at another. It is a fact of life too that if one can't laugh at oneself, one may be missing the best joke around! The philosophy of this assertion is confirmed by St Teresa of Avila's advice, 'Don't take yourself seriously; take God seriously!'

Conscious of the immense fund of common sense in the outlook of St Teresa, I must say that the current ruling from Rome outlawing the use of 'inclusive language' (i.e. 'she', 'her', or 'sisters') amuses me no end, especially when I read of gracious canonised women saints described as 'Fathers of the Church', if you don't mind! Exclusion of 'inclusive language', whatever else it does, certainly does not assist in clarity of expression for the ordinary Catholics of today.

In this connection, I gladly and gratefully remember a friend of mine, Eamon, who, possessing one of the sharpest and keenest intellects I have ever known always rubbished clumsy, inexact expressions. When seeking to establish with him the meaning of certain passages and expressions of mutual interest, having listened to his lucid explanations, I might observe, 'Eamon, maybe he (or she) meant ...' It always provoked the instant and withering response, 'Andy, why can't people say and write what they mean?' Easier said than done apparently, particularly if one is constrained by present Roman rulings restricting the use of certain words. To his eternal credit, one retired parish priest, now in his mid-eighties, when leading the congregation at Sunday Mass in the recitation of the Creed, always intones emphatically, 'For us and for our salvation ...' refusing to follow the script in the official Mass leaflet, 'For us men and our salvation ...' In doing so, he honours 50% (more nowadays) of the congregation present, with my whole spirit rejoicing, especially when my wife, daughters, daughter-in-law, ladies in the Church's Healing Ministry, girl altar servers, female Ministers of the Word and the Eucharist, all give a deeper, fuller appreciation of Church.

Seriously though, where does the present spectacle of women's role in the Church today leave the teaching of St Paul, enshrined in Scripture? What are we to make of his words, for instance, that it would be inconceivable that a woman's voice be heard in Church? We should never forget, however, that he came from Judaism, one of whose regulations ensured that females were strictly precluded from worshipping with males in the Temple, the fair sex being confined to its outer section. We must never forget either that in St Paul's day, the accepted order of society deemed that not alone were women regarded as nothing; rather they were classified as less than nothing! And into such a society was Jesus Christ born!

More confusion follows when we realise that St Paul is considered to be the greatest interpreter ever of Christianity. It certainly appears that such a claim must now be qualified and modified in relation to his view and understanding (or lack of it!) of the role of women in God's creation and in the Church. We must also understand that St Paul was absolutely certain that the second coming of Christ (i.e. the Last Day) would happen in his life time, as were the Apostles. We know now that Paul was wrong and so was the whole infant Church in this particular teaching, the more years going by without it happening, adding to their embarrassment. Naturally then, when the first century AD was drawing to a close, the Church had to quietly forget this widely held doctrine, but like every other organisation and everyone else, it had to live with the consequences of the mistake. How then does one view the magesterium of the Church in the light of these undeniable facts of history in the distant past and in the not too distant past? All I can say at this juncture is that it is no help at all to pretend that these things did not happen. We may conclude, however, that St Paul had no conception at all of the future, for his philosophy of the function and place of females in the Church was contradicted totally by the establishment of religious orders of contemplative and semi-contemplative sisters, centuries after the coming of Christ. I'm not in the least impressed either when I read of celibate men trying to explain why inclusive language is unacceptable in the Catholic Church. Obviously they are light years removed from the position of Catholic married lay men endeavouring to justify this same exclusion to their wives! Not all of the first priests ordained at the Last Supper were celibate; we cannot deny that at least one of their number, St Peter, was married. Therefore, it would appear that this particular Scripture cannot be quoted in defence of the refusal of the Church to ordain married men. Truly, we ignore history at our peril.

The official Church's attitude to women generally has always amazed me when we consider that the first person to be informed after the promise of centuries, that the Messiah was about to appear on the earth in human form, was a woman, the Blessed Virgin Mary. We know too that under the cross of Jesus at Calvary, women outnumbered men three to one. Every Christian is also aware that the validity of the faith hangs on one slender thread – Resurrection – for if Christ be not risen, the faith is in vain. When the Resurrection happened, however, we read in St Mark's Gospel chapter 16, verse 9, that Christ did not immediately contact Peter, James, John, Andrew or indeed any of the Apostles. Significantly he first appeared to a woman, Mary of Magdala! So, a woman knew that Christ was risen before the first Pope became aware of it!

Women were at the centre of many of the spectacular miracles of Jesus Christ too. Martha was at his side when, by the power of the Living Word, Jesus raised her brother from the dead, four days after his death. A widowed mother saw her only son on his way to burial, raised from the dead by the power of Jesus Christ. A girl possessed by a demon was delivered when her mother implored Jesus to set her daughter free. When the woman caught in the act of adultery was brought to Jesus for condemnation (had the guy involved no responsibility?), the Lord knelt and began writing in the dust of the road. His action scattered that all-male, accusing assembly, the mob dispersing silently, led by the eldest. The only Man left there was Jesus Christ and astonishingly we know that He was kneeling, with Scripture telling that Jesus looked up before addressing the woman.

One of the most detailed accounts of a one to one encounter found in the Gospels is the story of Jesus approaching a lone woman at a well, His action amazing the Apostles. Again, one of the earlier miracles of Jesus happened when He found Peter's mother-in-law suffering from a fever. This healing was so stunningly instant that the Gospel tells of her rising to begin serving a meal to her son-in-law's distinguished visitor and friends. The first person raised from the dead by Jesus was the daughter of Jarius. Then, there was the woman Anna at the centre of the beautiful story of the Presentation of Jesus in the Temple, with the man on the reception committee there ruining the joy of the occasion by forecasting bad news to the Mother and Infant. Talk about bad timing! Trust a man to spoil things! Why had he to disclose the bad news at all? Even allowing that he specifically knew the future, what good did it do? If this suffering was inevitable, why not leave it to unfold in its own good time? Was Simeon a father himself? How would he react should an uninvited bystander arrive at the shining hour of a solemn religious ritual celebrating the birth of his son and announce doom and gloom prospects for the mother of his child? Whatever gifts Simeon had, discretion was not one of them. By now, you can gather that Simeon is not one of my favourite characters in the Gospels – not by a long shot!

We notice too on Resurrection Day that the women who ministered to Christ during His public life rose at daybreak to go to His grave to attend to His mortal remains as they thought. I presume the Apostles stayed in bed or remained indoors, fearful that they would suffer the same fate as their Master. Nearing the grave the women saw a vision of angels, one of whom shocked them by asking why they were seeking a Living Man among the dead. Although this entirely unexpected confrontation with the Angel of the Resurrection frightened the wits out of them, the undisputed fact is that the ladies knew Christ had risen before the Apostles, from whom the all-male College of Cardinals in the Church is descended. Even when the ultimate act of redemption, Pentecost, occurred, with the Holy Spirit descending in the form of tongues of fire on each person in that little assembly, huddled together behind closed and locked doors, it must have been a mixed congregation. We know as much, for in Acts of the Apostles chapter 1, verse 14 we learn of the Apostles devoting themselves to prayer together with the women and Mary, the Mother of Jesus. Then, in Acts 2, we read that when the day of Pentecost arrived, they were all together in one place so we can assume that the ladies were there too. With the fair sex so visibly present in the story of redemption (and so necessary too!) I often ponder that should all references to women be deleted from each of the four Gospels, what kind of documents would we be left with? If it were so, then these accounts would not reflect God's entire creation. How blessed the whole Church is that inclusive language was not outlawed when these narratives were written. It obviously posed no problems for the authors, so for the life of me I can't fathom why it is necessary to complicate things in modern Church printed matter.

I listened recently to a bishop commenting on Church affairs generally and not alone did he deplore the hurt inflicted on 50% of God's creatures by the absence of feminine terminology in the liturgy and in other official Church publications but advanced the view that the world-wide decline of religious orders of nuns is a far greater threat to the Church than the fall in vocations to the priesthood. The bishop appreciated and identified those who work at the coal face of evangelisation – and they are not men!

How strange it is that in this chapter, starting out to explore our Christian faith, I quickly and unexpectedly focused on such a serious and controversial topic as the status of women in the Church. But returning to the joyful side of our religion, I'm reminded of a friend of mine, Mary, who with her spouse organised a 'bash' for family and friends to celebrate their fortieth wedding anniversary. Very late in the evening, with the party 'flying', a priest friend dropped in and, when asked to bless the cake, innocently enquired of the bride of forty years, 'Maybe in honour of the occasion you might like to renew now your marriage vows?' Mary's lightning-like reaction was to exclaim, 'No bloody way, Father!' In the resulting uproar of laughter no one could remember whether or not the cake was ever blessed with the happy couple so convulsed with the joy of it all being quite unable to even attempt to hold the knife together. To really appreciate the humour of this story, one would need to be married for 40 years or longer, I guess! I can guarantee too that all the verbal expressions at this joyful celebration were utterly inclusive!

I find it extremely difficult to tease out views of young people today on Church difficulties, for the simple reason that so many of them are turned off completely by religion. Parents galore, themselves solid and practising Catholics, tell of their offspring dropping basic religious practices like attendance at Sunday Mass, as soon as they leave the nest. Also in areas of Dublin city with unemployment rates running to 70% plus it is par for the course to find the vast majority of men opting out of Sunday Mass too. A Dublin based priest with an interest in sociology recently did a survey in one disadvantaged parish of my adopted city and found men who refused to attend Sunday Mass, because, in their own words, 'God closed our factories. He is not mindful of us, so why should we bother?' Love it or leave it, call it naive or simplistic if you wish, but that is what these unemployed people are saying, with many families experiencing a second generation of workless members. As everyone knows, unemployment is the greatest social evil facing the European Union, with Ireland having the unenviable distinction of topping the unemployment league in this far flung community of nations.

Sadly too, all the Christian Churches in Europe seem powerless in the face of this horrible ordeal for their people and should our religious leaders and institutions continue to be so ineffective, helpless and useless, in the face of this massive trial there is a grave danger that the new generation leaving schools and colleges in the final years of this century will write off all organised religions as irrelevant, a harmless occupation for the aged. Continually offering young people 'pie in the sky' only is just not on nowadays.

In such an atmosphere I thank God for the Charismatic Renewal movement as at least at these weekly meetings something concrete, visible and meaningful is on offer. There, people see and hear of physical healings regularly by the power of the Holy Spirit when hands are laid on the sick. At these gatherings too people are encouraged to pray aloud for the cure of their economic ills and by the power of the same Spirit, many petitions of this nature are regularly answered with many of these success stories recorded in my books for all to read. At Renewal meetings, the Word of the Living God is presented as something practical, a power which really works and is seen to do so in the lives of ordinary people. Furthermore, the congregation is actually invited to base their prayers on the Word when seeking help in marital difficulties, for instance when infertility looms or when the curse of alcoholism wreaks havoc in families. Even single people find partners in marriage through Scriptural prayer; why not, as with God nothing is impossible. How thrillingly attractive and contagiously joyful it is to witness people publicly, unashamedly and lucidly, personally testifying to various healings and cures while thanking the Lord for these very visible graces. Maybe the Charismatic Renewal movement is shouting at the structured Church to sit up and take notice of a role model of what may prove to be the universally accepted Church of Jesus

Christ in the world in the near future. If you think this is a new idea, then think again because it was a man named St Paul who declared the Kingdom of God is not just words, it is power. But don't take my word for it; look it up for yourself in 1 Corinthians, chapter 4, verse 20.

As I said previously, it is extraordinary how in this chapter, I have been continually led away from discussing glad tidings. I suppose it shows how difficult it is for Christians to constantly live in the joy of the Lord. What may not be surprising is that so much of this chapter focused on the fair sex. Actually for me, whatever the philosophers may conclude, a good definition of hell on earth is a world without women! Come to think of it, if things were so, how could I have been born?

However, joyful surprises tend to regularly arise when one endeavours to walk with the Holy Spirit as the following story illustrates. One evening when I called to a nursing home to visit a friend, I nipped into the oratory there to say a quick prayer when a cleric passed by, walking smartly, slapping an evening paper against his knee. When he sat down in a pew near me, the humour of our situation struck me, so I rose and genuflected, but before leaving, approached this priest and, trusting that he had a developed sense of humour, whispered, 'Excuse me Father, but seeing you carrying an evening paper, I couldn't help thinking, "there's a man with the bad news whereas I have the Good News!"', as I showed him a small Bible I was carrying! He took a deep breath, smiled and replied very humbly and sincerely, 'Thanks; I needed that!'

I then introduced myself, explained that I was there to visit a friend, and extended my hand in greeting. He took my hand, held it and repeated my name three times, seemingly in wonder, before exclaiming, 'Don't tell me you are the man who writes the books on healing!'

Dumbfounded, I replied, 'My goodness, have you read them?'

'I haven't,' was his response, as he observed, 'but strangely, one of my priests gave me a book of yours an hour ago. I'll begin reading it tonight!'

It was only at that moment that I caught sight of the flash

of purple beneath his Roman collar, as he revealed, 'I'm Bishop "X"'.

Instantly I responded, 'I wouldn't have come near you with a 40 foot pole, my lord, if I had known you were a bishop!'

I listened as he explained that he was a patient in the nursing home and astonishingly heard him ask, 'Now that I know you lay hands on the sick, will you please do so to me?'

Amazingly and unexpectedly, I found myself laying hands on a man on whom the fullness of the priesthood had been conferred, as this lovely man joined his hands and bowed his head like a seven year-old boy on his First Holy Communion Day. With a deep sense of reverence, I placed my hands on his shoulders and said a short healing prayer based on chapter 4 of the Letter of St James and concluded by requesting him to bless my hands which I lay on the sick. He did so, then, slowly and very warmly, we shook hands, I wished him well and left, consoled by the knowledge that my hands had now been blessed by seven bishops in Ireland, England, Scotland and in the United States.

Christians should expect the joy of the Lord to constantly surface in their lives. It must do, because Jesus Christ Himself said, 'I am the light of the world'. Therefore, the Christian faith must have its inner moments, as the God whom Christians worship as being infinite must have an infinite sense of humour too. The Healing Ministry of the Holy Church is not without its laughs either for if it was all unrelieved doom and gloom, the drop-out rate of those involved would be enormous. This joy, fun and laughter strongly surfaces in the most unexpected places and often concerns people surrounded by unbelievable sorrow as the following story vividly demonstrates.

Mary was a born and bred Londoner who met John when he emigrated from Ireland to the UK. They fell in love, married and settled down in England's capital city, but John always yearned to return to his roots. Life on the land called him, as in no way was he attracted to working in industry. Eventually, they arrived in the west of Ireland, bought a small parcel of arable land and set up farming in a very modest way. Both of them worked hard and they were blessed with three children. When their eldest child was fifteen, John took suddenly ill and found himself at 40 years of age in hospital for the first time ever. Within one month he was given the death sentence, the prognosis being that he had no more than six months to live.

Husband and wife were understandably shattered and at this frightfully traumatic time in their life, Mary sought help at her nearest Charismatic Renewal prayer meeting. On reading my books, she rang me and as I was wont to do, I encouraged her to continue attending her meeting every week and suggested that she read Scripture daily. Finally, on the understanding that my prayer is as effective or as ineffective as the next person's (for confirmation of this assertion see Galatians chapter 2, verse 6), I prayed with Mary, seeking recovery for her husband. Some weeks later, seemingly at her request and as a last resort, John was transferred to St Vincent's Hospital, Dublin for a second opinion, but alas, there was no joy for them, with the consultants there confirming the prognosis of their colleagues. At Mary's request, I visited John twice while he was in Dublin and it was obvious that he was a very sick man. Shortly afterwards he was transferred to the hospital in the north-west of Ireland, where within weeks, John sadly died.

Mary suddenly found herself alone, a Londoner with a young family on a small holding in a foreign country, her culture shock and grief being both unimaginable and indescribable. In the short run, a farm had to be worked and managed while children, numb with terror and shock, had to be comforted and supported, somehow, someway. No wonder Mary cried from the depth of her misery, 'Why, Oh God, why?' When she rang me, I hadn't any answers. Neither had anyone else. All I could do, I did, listening to her when she rang, being physically present to her during her calls as despite it all, through it all, I even dared to pray with her. Whether or not this religion business made any sense or meaning to her at that time in Mary's life, I didn't know, but I had nothing else to offer. Many times after these phone sessions I asked myself why in God's name did I ever get mixed up in this Healing Ministry as I even questioned the validity of the name.

I do though remember one call from Mary which was unexpectedly different. Of course she expressed, as usual, her grief through tears, but out of the blue she mentioned that her belief in the existence of angels had been renewed! Sensing her comment was beyond me, she quickly explained, 'I'm not seeing visions Andy, but two angels materialised in my life when John died, and didn't I need them?' These Heavenly bodies were certainly solid and substantial, it transpired, on standing at 6 feet 4 inches and weighing 14 stones, the other being his good wife – Mary's neighbour whose land adjoins hers. Without invitation or fuss, they presented themselves in Mary's farm, helped with the milking of the cows, advised her in relation to milk testing and could forecast within hours when a cow would calf.

The little cockney girl born within the sound of Bow Bells could never have imagined the pattern of life would lead her from London town, with its teeming millions, to this utterly strange environment of Ireland's north-western seaboard. Then, wonder of wonders, I heard the sound of laughter from Mary for the first time ever, as she enquired if I knew anything about herding cows! Coming from generations of townsfolk, I had to confess my complete ignorance as I listened to what happened when she and her two angel minders were herding the cows from grazing to the milking parlour on that same evening. One cow proved to be contrary, would not walk with the herd and at long last broke free and ran for a gap. Mary stopped dead still in the middle of the field and shouted, 'Dear God, grant that she may turn to her left!' Neither God nor the cow paid any heed to her plea, however, the cow went through the gap, turned right and disappeared from view behind a hedgerow leading Mary to exclaim in exasperation, 'Good God! Don't tell me you don't know your left from your right!' Not alone did I enjoy a good belly laugh with Mary, I took pleasure in it, with my heart rejoicing, knowing that she was winning. I knew now that she and her family would survive, with her phone call plainly indicating that she was not going to surrender to self-pity or allow herself to be destroyed by excessive grief even though she might be unconscious of making these life-saving decisions. Symbolically and significantly, I never heard from Mary again and may it be joy all the way for that good woman for the rest of her life. God knows she deserves it.

Life for all is a mixture of sunshine and showers and maybe the survival route is, by God's grace, to look forward to the sunshine when the showers come as we travel towards eternity where St Paul assures us that tears are no more, interpreting His Divine Master's consoling word that as the Father has prepared nothing less than a kingdom for His followers, they should never be fearful during life's journey. I am quite convinced though if our lifestyle in religion or out of it has succeeded in banishing laughter, then we should pull over to the hard shoulder of the road, stop the car, check the road map and the traffic signs and make sure that we are on course for our destination. Should there be no sound of laughter, the probability is that we have missed a major turn and are heading into a cul-de-sac.

How relaxing life is too when one accepts the freedom to laugh at one's self. You don't agree? Read on and be converted! During my business career, I attended Mass in Our Lady's Oratory in Dublin's Leeson Street before beginning my day's work in my offices nearby. One morning outside this church in my very early days in Renewal, I was confronted by an old lady. She had difficulty walking, carried a stick and instantly blurted out, 'I hear you're charismatic!' Next, before I could gather my wits, she continued, 'I'm sorry to hear that – I'm rheumatic!' and then enquired casually, 'What clinic do you attend?' I assure you, this story is not fictional, and re-telling it has brought joy and laughter to many in Ireland and abroad, particularly to those in Renewal circles. This type of story helps immeasurably in promoting a light-hearted approach to the spiritual life too, as I can't for the life of me see how one can spread the Good News with a face that would frighten the crows, stop a clock or a runaway horse!

5

BUSINESS, ALCOHOL AND CHARISMATIC RENEWAL

In my student days, I recall one of the lecturers describing economic life as human life. I also know that striving to earn a living, endeavouring to make one's fortune, battling to get to the top of the heap and to stay there in life's various disciplines and activities, tends to bring out the best in some people and the worst in others. The rat race, jungle law, the killer instinct, the survival of the fittest, the unacceptable face of capitalism and the dog eat dog mentality, are not empty phrases, with some people now prepared to kill opponents to gain a desired goal. Why, I even heard a very shrewd business analyst describing cold-bloodedly a managing director of a prominent company as 'a merciless animal to work for!' Naturally it was an off the cuff, not for publication, private one to one comment with the law of libel the way it is, but it was a claim which would not be disputed in business circles. Therefore this tough helter-skelter, 100 miles an hour competitive winner-takes-all environment presents an enormous challenge to those who strive to be as successful as possible while conforming to Christian principles.

When I first entered management I found myself the recipient of much advice and was given copious hints and tips as to how to be a success. One of the most outrageous pieces of advice given to me during this very special time in my career as I sought to come to terms with my new responsibilities was, 'If at any one time half your staff is not calling you a dictator, then you are not managing!' Without hesitation I instantly rejected this proposition, knowing that there had to be a better way.

There was, and I found it, but that's a story for another day.

Be that as it may, the true story which unfolds in this chapter concerns Roy, who, seeing a hole in the market, left his permanent pensionable job at 25 years of age and started business on his own. The familiar one-liner that to be a success in the market-place one must initially have 'a bit of pluck and bit of luck', was certainly true of Roy as he had lots of both. His unstoppable energy, dedication, ability to work long hours plus a high IQ, a great pair of hands, rock steady nerves and vulgar physical health brought him and his company to a position among the top organisations in his field after a quarter of a century of sustained effort.

Then suddenly, disaster struck through Alex, a most important client and trusted customer of long standing. Alex settled his account on two-monthly intervals by special arrangement and never failed to meet his commitments even when recessionary times arrived. However, one fateful morning, instead of the expected cheque in the post, Roy received a phone call from Alex who explained that he had a temporary cash crisis. As he was receiving Alex's phone call, Roy's credit controller silently indicated that a sum well in excess of a £250,000 was due, information which was truly more than sufficient to concentrate Roy's mind on every syllable uttered by the caller. Alex explained the reasons for his temporary cash flow interruption and, without beating about the bush, sought a further month's extension. Needless to say, it was the prelude to a long, stressful confrontation between these two seasoned business campaigners, but as Alex was one of Roy's best and biggest customers with an impeccable track record of payment, reluctantly Roy acceded to the request.

Within a split second of the ending of their conversation, the scene in Roy's office dramatically changed, resembling the command centre of a warship on active service when the 'Active stations – enemy sighted' siren shrieks throughout the ship, with Roy, his sales manager, credit controller and accountant feverishly examining Alex's pattern of orders and payments. This exercise necessitated the cancelling of all their business appointments for that day, with their deliberations lasting well into the evening. Resulting from this meeting, in effect, one of the tools of survival in the business world, industrial espionage, extensively used though rarely mentioned, was set in motion, one way or another, with each of this four man team being assigned separate tasks. When they eventually scattered and headed home, not a single word of that meeting was recorded nor was their meeting resumed. Over the next fortnight, Alex was first checked out against the three d's – drink, drugs and dames, without anything surfacing nor was there any evidence of gambling at racetracks. His credit ratings originally submitted to Roy were critically re-examined with nothing of significance arising there either. His business premises and offices were 'cased' for any signs of panic but no signals were picked up, nor was there any gossip forthcoming when pubs, clubs, 'nite spots' and golf clubs were trawled.

Meanwhile the month dragged on as Roy sweated it out with every working day beginning with verbal reports as Alex's position was reviewed from every possible angle. At last the first day of the new month dawned with Roy anxiously awaiting his business post and naturally when this special delivery arrived it was hastily scanned. Alas, there was no communication from Alex. Reacting, Roy reached for his phone and rang Alex's office, only to be told that he was away for some days while an answering machine prevented any contact with him at his home. Two days later Roy was shattered by the news that a receiver had been appointed to Alex's company. Alex was bankrupt! Immediately, a damage limitation exercise was launched by Roy whose primary object was now to survive. Alex's very considerable debt with the loss of this major account could have seriously damaged his company with Roy reckoning he needed immediate temporary accommodation for a sum in the region of £500,000, to keep afloat. This proposition certainly separated the men from the boys among the financial institutions who live by loaning funds to the corporate sector. Eventually Roy was successful, even allowing that it cost an arm and a leg interest-wise and necessitated surrendering the deeds of his business premises as collateral. After 25 years of slogging, he was almost back to scratch and although grateful to be still in business, he had to admit that he had suffered a severe shock. Roy, recognising that he was no longer a young man, realised that he could not repeat either the pace or the long hours of work which built up his organisation. Instead, he put his head down, ruled out all recreation, refused to surrender to self-pity and was determined to maintain the quality of life for himself and his clan. A beautiful home, two cars, children at private schools, prominent in his golf club with an accepted niche in Dublin's commercial world was more than sufficient to fuel his motivation.

Roy did, though, make one concession to this seven-day week, work to bed routine, by faithfully attending his weekly Charismatic Renewal meeting, where surprisingly, after some weeks he was presented with a dilemma with Alex at its core. With the news filtering through from the receiver, Roy was initially informed that he might receive the money due to him after six months, the next payment was postponed to twelve months, with Roy endeavouring to come to terms with the grim truth that he was chasing a lost cause. Detestation of and bitterness towards Alex were now eating into Roy who soon found himself uncomfortable singing the Lord's prayer at the conclusion of the prayer meeting, the petition, 'as we forgive those who trespass against us', causing the unease. This Christian principle, while seemingly harmless in theory, was proving to be impossible in practice. How could he be expected to forgive Alex? It also dawned on Roy that not alone had he to forgive Alex, but he was actually expected to love him! Logically he concluded that he was first and forever precluded from doing any further business with Alex in the unlikely event of Alex ever again entering the ranks of business, unless he presented his order with a guaranteed cheque. Second, should he ever be requested to supply a business reference for Alex, he would have to spell out the unsavoury facts, the laws of justice, natural and divine, his conscience and one of the fundamental gifts of the Holy Spirit, common sense, all precluding any other alternative. Roy always accepted that God was not praised by stupid and imprudent business practices, therefore, turning away from resentment towards Alex, forgiving him for the injury he inflicted, while finally coming to accept him as a brother in Christ, seemed a three span bridge too far.

Out of the blue then, while driving home alone after a prayer meeting, Roy found himself toying with the idea of praying for Alex! After six months of unrelenting business pressure and torment, it seemed a preposterous proposition. He drove into his driveway and, ever a naturally gifted and swift decision-maker, grabbed his Bible, opened it at Psalm 20 and prayed it for Alex! It was a routine that Roy repeated every evening in his car when he arrived home. A month or so later, everything began to turn round for him in his business. Strain and stress seemed to leave Roy and he even found himself out to dinner with his wife one Friday evening. There he met friends, and astonishingly heard himself accepting an invitation to play golf on the following Sunday morning!

It was at this stage that Roy rang me and unfolded his story, emphasising that since he opened his Scripture and prayed Psalm 20 for Alex and continued to do so daily, untold blessings came his way. Primarily, he gladly revealed that he was no longer 'in the red' – he had come through the ordeal unscathed mentally and physically and his marriage was never better. Next, he asserted that he now had personal experience of the awesome power released when one prays the Lord's prayer and receives the grace to apply it to the circumstances of life, the implications of its seven petitions. Finally, and more importantly though, Roy disclosed that he was now free of the burden of Alex, realising yet again, that life is for living, where people go round only once, so it is not a dress rehearsal. Roy was no longer imprisoned by the memories of the past. He signed off with, 'Thank you for Charismatic Renewal. Now we can make sense of the hustle and bustle around us while keeping our eye on the main chance – the next life. We must have a game of golf soon, Andy.'

Speaking of golf reminds me of another businessman that I met casually when seeking exercise and fresh air, I decided to go golfing and found myself in the locker room of my club very early one Monday morning. There was only one other man there, so we introduced ourselves and as neither of us were fixed up with partners we went out together. He rejoiced in the name of Bill (there are no titles on golf courses), had a 'Green Fees Paid' sticker on his golf bag and was from the United States, attending a business conference in Dublin. Furthermore, he explained that as he had arranged to be picked up by taxi, he would have to quit our game after two hours, irrespective of the state of play. It was an arrangement that suited me fine.

As we made our way to the first tee, surprisingly he ruled out any discussion on handicaps, saying, 'I'm not a serious golfer any more; I just play for the fun and the fresh air'. I gave him the honour of driving off and noticed that he had an adequate and relaxed swing, as both of us matched par. He was by no means a young man and, walking to the second tee, he expounded, 'I've cut out all pressure from my life, on and off golf courses. I had to, as I nearly killed myself.' Walking down the second fairway following our drives, in an unexpected burst of confidence, he confided, 'Andy, over the last three years I went to the brink of eternity, falling into the hands of coronary specialists, psychologists and psychiatrists. Why, I even spent time in the Mayo clinic. The end result is that I now abide by four specific laws of life. To discover this survival plan cost me a king's ransom but I'll disclose it to you for nothing.' We played our approach shots, holed out and went to the next tee, as I wondered what I had let myself in for when he disclosed that he was president of a group of insurance companies, of all businesses! To get to the top of the heap, he had subjected himself to an unbelievably punishing routine for over four decades, working a 16 hour, six day week, only meeting his wife and children on Sundays! Birthdays and anniversaries were always held on the Sabbath day to accommodate him while he invariably opted out of family holidays.

Bill inevitably had a complete collapse, beginning when he fell to the floor, presiding over a full board meeting of his associated companies, was stretchered unconscious from his palatial penthouse suite of offices in a towering New York skyscraper to be admitted to the Intensive Care Unit of a private clinic. At this stage of our game I almost thought that I was at the movies rather than on a golf course, but it all came together for me at a par 5 hole. I unleashed a massive drive, the ball soared up and away straight down the middle, comfortably cleared the stream which dissects this down-hill fairway, as with immense satisfaction I realised that I was in a perfect position for my second shot. With a good lie, I next hit a towering Number 1 wood shot, with the ball astonishingly finishing on the edge of the rolling green. The adrenaline was now flowing so I stepped up with my putter and with Jack Nicklaus-like confidence, unerringly sank the fifteen yard putt, my whoop of triumph signalling that I had achieved the first eagle of my golfing life. Delightedly, I exclaimed, 'Bill, everyone is entitled to a quarter of an hour of fame in a lifetime!' as he holed out, struggling to keep an eight off his card.

After my 'miracle score', I assumed that he would become slightly more interested in the golf but, discovering that adjacent to our next tee stood one of Dublin's well-known hospitals, gave my companion the opportunity to outline his first law of life. It was a crisp four word one-liner – 'An apple a day', dictating moderation in food intake, irrespective of season or celebration, strict limitation of alcohol with a complete exclusion of smoking. Five minutes and two shots later, I discovered his second law – 'A walk in the fresh air, alone, for an hour every day', as, standing perfectly still on the cherry blossom tree-lined fairway on that magnificent spring morning, Bill, authoritatively warned, 'Andy, the Man who made time made plenty of it – 24 hours every day. Therefore if I can't find time to spend one hour each day relaxing and strolling with the person I get on best with in life – myself – then I'm badly organised.' With finger wagging he added, 'I don't need to labour the point that where one finds disorganisation, there lies chaos and confusion, leading to stress, that universal destroyer of life.'

The third law of life quickly followed and was another one-liner – 'Learn to say "No"' – its philosophy presenting a massive challenge to Bill as it contradicted and confronted his whole behaviour pattern up to the moment. He reviewed his life after regaining consciousness in hospital. Bill recalled when the opportunity to work over-time first presented itself in his career, how enthusiastically he said 'Yes'. How else could a person become a success? It became an ingrained habit and was his constant companion as he rose in the ranks. So few could match his blistering pace that he soon burned off all competitors, channelling every surplus dollar earned into stocks and shares. On the Stock Exchange, Bill always led the charge of those prepared to gamble on high risk ventures and as a consequence was more than willing to pay the price of sleepless nights. Realising that money was the key to power, Bill spent every waking hour accumulating it, saying 'Yes' to everything and everybody who might be of use to him is his insatiable thirst for more.

Bill founded his own company and many more in the following years, eventually basking in the title of 'Mr President'. Lying in bed, staring at a white hospital ceiling while a heart monitor ticked away at his side was, however, a whole new ball game for this middle-aged man as he endeavoured to come to terms with life now that his hands were divorced from the comforting grip of telephones. Bill truly saw himself though as a wounded lion, when, on his discharge to the recovery ward, he found a psychologist of all people sitting by his bedside. At 61 years of age, he was learning to say 'No', accepting that failure to obey the new rules would at best lead him to a psychiatrist's couch and at worst summarily usher him into the next life. Why, only a month previously, how well he now recalled his inability to say 'No' when advised by senior board members to delegate much of his responsibilities.

We completed our round of golf comfortably within his two hour target, shook hands and, heading towards the club house, he made the sign of the cross, while smilingly observing, 'That's the fourth law of life for me, Andy – make the sign of the cross regularly each day'. He went on, 'Life in New York, in the market place, in the streets and in the home is so unpredictable and surrounded as we are with mindless violence, I now accept as a Christian our struggle in life is not against human forces only, but against evil powers as St Paul warns.

So I make the sign of the cross many times during the day for protection, even after a game of golf.' As he spoke, I noticed that he looked meditatively across the fairway at the hospital building in the distance. At the club house, we shook hands again and he gave me his business card saying, 'Any time you find yourself in the Big Apple, give me a call, Andy,' adding impishly, 'But I'm only available during normal business hours!' With these words, 'Mr President', he walked right out of my life.

Love them or leave them, Bill's four laws of life are certainly working for him, demonstrating too that there is no conflict whatsoever between common sense and basic Christian values; rather they complement each other. Thought provoking also to contemplate that two businessmen, Roy and Bill, had each relied heavily on Christian faith to survive in time of crisis, one in the old world, the other in the new world, as they both travel inexorably to the next world, with the rest of us for company.

IT IS NOW AN historical fact that miracles of every kind and description are constantly witnessed at the Charismatic Renewal prayer meeting in 'Avila' Carmelite Monastery, Dublin with my various books on healing recording these happenings for both present and future generations.

One evening a mature man arrived at this prayer meeting, alone, sat down and neither spoke to nor recognised anyone present. Actually Val, one of the stewards, thought he dozed off through the best part of the service. When the meeting ended he became somewhat more alert and proceeded to move with the crowds heading for the prayer room where the laying on of hands ceremony is held. He was prayed with there and nodded his head in thanks as Val noticed him wandering out of the monastery. Almost two years later the same man arrived in 'Avila' again, now looking very much with it. Val instantly recognised him, welcomed him and recalled the circumstances of his first visit too, whereupon the man revealed his experience on that evening. 'I don't remember much of the prayer meeting,' he explained, 'but I recall standing before a lady who laid her hands on my shoulders. I can honestly say, though I only saw her through an alcoholic haze!'

The following morning he woke up, got out of bed and amazingly decided that his drinking days were over! Realising that he could do with all the help that he could get, this former chronic alcoholic contacted Alcoholics Anonymous and not alone has been on the 'dry' since but is actively involved with that organisation in assisting others afflicted with the curse of alcoholism.

Studying this man's story, first, one can assume that the lady in 'Avila', when he stood before her, must have unhesitatingly sought from the Lord the gift of sobriety for him. She could hardly have done anything else as he must have smelt like a brewery in full production! Second, how blessed he was to know that in 'Avila' at the Charismatic Renewal prayer meeting, he could, without any fuss, prior appointment or loss of dignity, mingle anonymously with a crowd seeking healing of all kinds. Significantly enough, apart from the Charismatic Renewal prayer movement, I don't know of any other vehicle in the Catholic Church today where such a necessary service is so readily available to afflicted people. Third, in any detailed enquiry aimed at discovering reasons why this man was delivered from the horror of alcoholism one must be conscious of the power of the praising of God in tongues.

To shift the burden of alcoholism (universally described by victims as 'a monkey on one's back') from a person, prayer in tongues constantly proves to be extraordinarily effective. In this context, we must accept that it is a fact of the spiritual life that alcoholism is part of the many facets of the kingdom of evil visible in the modern world. It respects neither class, creed, sex, colour, age or nationality; it afflicts those possessing the brightest intellects as well as the ignorant, with education or knowledge no match for its power. When confronted with a problem of the 'dark side of the moon' like alcoholism, for which there is no natural explanation, one is forced to accept that there is a supernatural explanation – of the wrong order. Therefore when the praising of God in tongues is used against it, as these sounds have no natural meaning, one trusts that the

Holy Spirit translates them, gives them to Jesus Christ for presentation to the Father in the manner proclaimed in Vatican II's Document on Prayer, the very latest and authentic teaching of the Holy Church. As all who attend 'Avila' know well, there is regular, prolonged and loud praising of God in tongues during the prayer meeting there. Could it be one solid reason why this Wednesday evening gathering continually produces healing of afflictions associated with the spirit of darkness; healings seen seldom if ever when other methods are employed? Certainly the man who wandered into 'Avila' and only saw it through an alcoholic haze would be the last to argue against such a conclusion. As in life generally, results speak louder than words.

AT THE AGE OF 23, Jason was street-wise, single, lived alone in a bedsit and loved life. He left school at fourteen, worked in supermarkets, take-aways and bars, eventually becoming a van delivery driver. Most weekends, he supported the black economy doing 'nixers' – working where income tax would not be deducted from the agreed wage. On the last weekend of August 1993 Jason was engaged in this 'moonlighting' activity at a venue an hour's drive from his base. On being paid in cash, after pub grub and a few drinks, he adjourned to a disco. There he met a girl – which was one of the objects of the exercise – and both of them danced and drank the night away. In the early hours of the morning, he offered to leave the girl home, giving a lift to another couple too. Jason and friends, in high spirits sang and chatted merrily on their way – this was the good life. Rounding a turn suddenly, they were flagged down at a police check where within minutes Jason failed the breathalyser test. He was arrested, brought to the nearest police station, gave a blood sample and, being deemed unfit to drive, rang his Mum, Mary, who arrived and drove him to the family home, in silence. At 3 a.m. on that particular Monday morning Mary would hardly accept that she was experiencing the joys of marriage and the blessings of children!

Life in the fast lane has the propensity to change dramatically with frightening rapidity, Jason was learning too. Within weeks a summons was duly served on Jason, so he arrived at the family home, telling his Mum that he was in trouble. The stakes couldn't be higher as, should he lose his driving licence in court, his job would automatically end.

Shortly after the serving of that summons, on the recommendation of a friend, Mary rang me, outlined the problem while candidly admitting that she didn't know what I could do or might do to assist her son in his predicament. As I normally do in such circumstances, for starters, I responded by pointing Mary to her nearest Charismatic Renewal prayer meeting and suggested that she attend there weekly to praise God for the needs of her son. Next, I recommended that she read with Jason from chapter 2 of St Luke's Gospel, the story of the finding of the child Jesus in the Temple, praying, 'Jesus lost. Jesus found. May the confusion and trouble in Jason's life be lost and peace and justice found and his job protected.' Finally, realising that Mary had no knowledge of the Charismatic Renewal movement, I mentioned my books to her. As it was then quite evident that the action I was advocating was a whole new scene for her, I didn't offer to pray with her, leaving the next move to the Holy Spirit.

Days later, Mary contacted me again; she was reading the Scripture, reciting daily the prayer that I suggested, found a prayer meeting and had bought my first book. But there was one snag – Jason, totally irreligious since he was fourteen, scoffed at the request to join her in prayer. 'That's your department, Mum,' he declared. I recalled for Mary the very sobering words for a Christian, in the Letter to the Hebrews, chapter 11, 'Without faith, it is impossible to please God', while accepting that for a baptised pagan like Jason, this was a meaningless warning. But for her consolation, I reminded Mary of the compensating Scripture in the Acts of the Apostles, where St Paul writes, 'Believe in the Lord Jesus Christ and you and your household will be saved'; a Word bringing comforting hope to Christian parents in the presence of atheistic offspring. How blessed Jason was, unknown to himself, to have parents who cherished and practised the faith of their fathers. Finally, when Mary asked for prayers for her son, I realised that Jason was coming before the courts on a very serious charge of drink driving. I hold that anyone who is drunk in charge of a car is a potential murderer; therefore I knew that Jason would be friendless in court. But I also knew that even if the whole world turned against him, he could rely on his Mum to stand by him. In that context, I prayed with Mary and ended by suggesting that she and her son stop for a split second at the door of the court and ask the Lord to go before them on their judgment day.

When next I heard from Mary, the case was over; this was her story. Jason was found guilty on all charges and, standing in the dock, heard the judge say that he was considering sending him to gaol and revoking his licence. However, before coming to a decision, he called for character references, if any. Jason was deeply humiliated, realising that his self-centred conduct had rebounded so badly and so publicly on his loved ones as he listened to letters read out from his family's parish priest and from local politicians, lauding their responsibilities and status in the community. Even a policeman, senior in age and service, stepped forward to praise Jason's parents. The convicted man just stood there as family values based on honesty, fear of the Lord and respect for the neighbour were proclaimed, a philosophy of life which Jason had both despised and reneged as unworthy of the macho image he projected. Now these time-honoured virtues of his family were his only defence against prison and economic disaster. Finally the solicitor apologised profusely for his client's behaviour, appealed to the judge to substitute a fine rather than a gaol sentence, while pointing out that as Jason had no skills other than driving, should he lose his licence, he would become almost unemployable.

There was silence in court as the colour drained from Jason. Then after what seemed an eternity, the judge mentioned the character references, noted the parents of the man in the dock had presented themselves personally in court despite their son's age, and considering it was a first offence, handed Jason a hefty fine and endorsed his licence, but warned that should he ever again stand before him on a similar charge, prison and the loss of this licence would automatically follow.

As he walked from the court, Jason couldn't feel the ground under his feet. At that moment, he could identify completely with the observation of a solicitor friend of mine. 'It is certainly one of life's most terrifying experiences to fall into the hands of the law.' Strangely, Jason's Mum confirmed the whole affair had matured her son immeasurably; why, he even grew spiritually, she maintained, being deeply impressed when she paused and let the Lord into the court before them.

Naturally I responded by saying that I hoped that her son had learned his lesson and now realises that should he offend again, he will find himself letting the Lord in before him to a prison cell! I trust she will express these sentiments to him to demonstrate that those who praise the Lord and might be labelled by Jason and his peers as Bible punchers, holy Marys and holy Joes, are not fools. Jason will certainly be thrice blessed should he also discover the immense difference between wisdom and being street-wise. Sadly for him, these 'pearls of great price' are rarely discovered in this area of operation after working hours. The pub and disco, now an integral part of the modern recreational scene at home and abroad, need a further extension, otherwise spiritual appetites will not be catered for. I couldn't help thinking that Jason, stopped in his tracks when his Mum insisted that he let the Lord into court before him, was having a similar experience as Saul on the road to Damascus about 2,000 years earlier. Maybe the same road lies ahead for Jason; after all, as the man said, there is nothing new under the sun.

AMONG THE SEVEN ELEMENTS of worship familiar to those in the Charismatic Renewal prayer movement is prophecy and although one of the gifts of the Holy Spirit, it never ceases to confuse and puzzle many people uninvolved in Renewal. Christianity has its roots deep in Judaism as we know that prophecy was an integral part of the worship of Yahweh by the chosen people. The history of the Jewish people covering many centuries is recorded in remarkable detail in the Old Testament of Scripture where we find prophecy abounds. Christians believe that Jesus Christ is the Messiah promised by

God the Father to His people after the fall of our first parents and this same Jesus Christ came primarily to do the Will of the Father thereby fulfilling the whole Law and the Prophets. One of the first definitive acts of Jesus Christ on His Resurrection Day is described in the Gospel of St Luke, chapter 24, verses 13–35 under the sub-heading, 'The road to Emmaus', where we read of Him opening the Scriptures to two of His disciples, being amazed at their slowness to believe the full message of the prophets that Christ should suffer and so enter into His glory, emphasising this teaching by beginning with Moses and going through all the Prophets. Prophecy is therefore part of the fundamental belief of Christians, a component of the very basis of such faith. Even Pope John Paul II recently expressed a deep wish that prophecy should be restored to the whole Church, thereby confirming, endorsing and supporting the entire concept of prophecy as practised and promoted by the Charismatic Renewal movement world-wide. In the present sacramental and devotional structure of the Catholic Church, however, it is difficult to see where prophecy could have the opportunity to bloom and grow.

In this context, the Charismatic Renewal movement is ideally suited to this purpose and as such fulfils its obligation by laying down guide lines whereby the validity or otherwise of prophecies which surface at its prayer meetings may be judged. These guide lines are both negative and positive. On the negative side, we find Charismatic Renewal prophecy is not concerned at all in foretelling the future, with 'doom and gloom' forecasts and dire warnings of disasters to come being firmly outlawed also. Valid prophecy according to Charismatic Renewal principles is not even remotely related to, nor has it any connection, good, or indifferent with, fortune telling, astrology, spiritualism or any kindred philosophies. So much then for the negative side of this much misunderstood gift of the Holy Spirit. Turning to the affirmative aspect of prophecy then, for it to be valid, first and always, it must be consoling, uplifting, joyful, peaceful, comforting and hopeful. Second, it should invariably be based on or reflect Scripture. Third, it must mirror the teachings of the Fathers of the Church. Fourth and finally for Charismatic Renewal prophecy, it is imperative for it to be clear and easy to understand so that those who hear it in prayer meetings can retain something from it to dwell on during their meditative private prayer time.

It is a mistake to hold that prophecy is, and must be, restricted to very special people. It can't be so, for it is one of the gifts of the Holy Spirit, given to the faithful to build up the Church, the Body of Christ. We must of course recognise the Church as composed of clergy, secular and regular, sisters and brothers in religious orders and lay people, male and female, an organism utterly inclusive, each individual differing only in function, all mutually complementary. Viewing the Church, it is equally important to understand that human beings, irrespective of status, are equal on two counts – in dignity, in that each possesses an immortal soul, and destiny, in that everyone is heading for an eternity of happiness, or the reverse, in a future life. Undoubtedly, no one is permanently assigned to life on the planet earth; every member of the human race is irrevocably on his or her way out of their present form of existence. Therefore the concept of Church cannot be fully understood in any other restricted or elitist form, nor can the term *populi dei* applied to lay people in the Church by Pope John XXIII be fully appreciated either in any narrow sense. Prelate and priest, saint and sinner, male and female, rich and poor, white, black, brown and yellow, whether academically qualified or not, all make up the colourful canvas of existence with Christians the world over for almost 2,000 years sharing the consoling belief in faith that Jesus Christ has come and redeemed them. It is in that context that Pope John II longed to see prophecy widespread in the Church and in highlighting this gift of the Holy Spirit he certainly wasn't breaking any new ground; rather he was re-affirming one of the oldest traditions of the Church.

Some of the earliest historical records are found in the books of the Old Testament of Scripture and in this respect the Book of Numbers is considered to have come into existence *circa* 1200 BC. Interestingly in chapter 11, verses 24–30 of this same book we learn that Moses venerated prophecy holding it to be of great importance in the lives of God's chosen people. In this same passage we read how Yahweh came down in the cloud that over-shadowed the Tent and took some of the Spirit on him and put it on 70 of the elders of the people whom Moses gathered there. These then prophesied. From this same Scripture we learn that prophecy was from the very beginning associated with the Holy Spirit. Furthermore, we learn of two men who had not gone to the Tent who also began to prophecy in the camp causing so much confusion among the Jews that Moses was asked to stop them doing so, but he instantly and resolutely refused. Actually Moses made his wishes known, expressing his earnest desire that he would dearly love Yahweh to give the Spirit of prophecy to all. This wish of the Father of the Jewish race expressed in the year 1200 BC was re-echoed by the present Holy Father of the Catholic Church in the year 1994 AD thereby indicating that prophecy was held over a span of more than 3,000 years as a sacred way for God's people to worship their Creator.

One of the first conclusions we draw from this body of truth is that prophecy, as promoted and practised by the Charismatic Renewal Movement world-wide, is certainly not an attempt to teach old dogs new tricks; rather it is an integral part of what was from the beginning, is now and ever shall be until the end of time (when there will be no need for it) an acceptable way for the faithful to express their belief and so build up the Body of Christ. It can be safely concluded too that just as the Charismatic Renewal movement was instrumental in renewing the age old practice of laying on of hands by lay people in the Church, the Renewal movement is also responsible for renewing the Holy Spirit's gift of prophecy among ordinary run-of-the-mill Catholics in the Church today. However, it is necessary at this point to emphasise that this type of prophecy is spoken at a very specific place and at a defined time, by those gathered at prayer meetings, in the traditional period of silence immediately following the praising of God in tongues, with this space in the meeting set apart to encourage the prophets. It is held in Renewal and confirmed by constant and widespread experience that the praising of God in tongues promotes prophecy. Those with the gift of prophecy will be people who most certainly will have a regular prayer time, both public and private, will be daily readers of the Word and who will constantly listen to and meditate on it. People with the gift of prophecy will be acutely aware also that the most powerful prayer for Christians is based on the Living Word of God. Finally, when they receive a prophetic word, before issuing it publicly at prayer meetings, they will test its authenticity or otherwise against the guide lines for valid prophecy already outlined.

Prophecy can come in many ways but normally it arrives when a person is at prayer or strives to increase the presence of the Lord. An entire prophetic word may instantly surface or one or two sentences could be received with other words or phrases added later. Usually one is mediating when prophecy comes so it can be safely held then that prophecy is born of meditation. I endeavour to set aside the last hour of each day for private prayer and recently, during one of these sessions, I had a unique experience when a series of sentences came to me. Strangely this passage, a form of words or collection of sentences, call it what you will, was as clear as if I was reading it on a monitor, so much so that I grabbed pen and paper and wrote it down, amazed at its clarity and unity. It read as follows:

Be gentle with yourself; do not judge yourself harshly.
Do not distress yourself over anything; it too will pass.
Do not disturb yourself by measuring your performance against others; accept yourself as you are.
By God's grace, work out your salvation as best you can.
Be at peace with yourself. Be at peace with your God; only then can you bring peace to others.
Strive to live constantly in the joy of the Lord; it will banish all intensity and stress.
Walking with the Holy Spirit empowers you to enter the new life; kingdom living, a foretaste of heaven itself.

Studying it at my leisure, I noticed that the passage had seven sentences, the number which denotes totality in the liturgy and in Scripture, while I realised also that it reflected part of Psalm 37 and 2 of the Beatitudes.

Therefore as regards its validity it passed the Scripture test with flying colours. I also realised that the whole spirit of the passage was comforting, consoling and joyfully quiet, as it promoted peace and joy, the first fruits of the Spirit. Furthermore there was a direct link between the second sentence of the prophecy and the teaching of St Teresa of Avila, which could be expected considering my long association with the Carmelite monks in their monastery where I attend the weekly Charismatic Renewal prayer meeting. The old adage, 'Show me your company and I'll tell you what you are', is apparently as true today as ever! So very quickly I concluded this seven sentence passage could safely be sent forth as prophecy.

Prophecy acts on two levels when it is issued at a Charismatic Renewal meeting. On the first level it is heard by the entire congregation and in the silence which follows the praising of God in tongues; therefore no one knows how many or how few identify with it. The second level on which prophecy operates is where a person retains it, meditates on it at private prayer time, receives some message from it and acts accordingly. But generally speaking the main function of prophecy is to support and encourage the people of God on their journey to their Heavenly home.

Another prophetic word I received in prayer is as follows:

My people, when you gather and praise My name,
When you worship me in tongues,
When you give and receive prophecy,
When you send forth My Living Word,
When you endeavour to break that Word among you,
When you confess and profess Me publicly by recounting
     how My Spirit is working in your lives,
And then ask My Father in My name, for your needs,
You will find these disciplines forever new.

Thus I have led you to the pearl of great price.
You have arrived.
You need go no further.
Here you will grow according to My plan for you.
When you persevere in this way, you will hear My Father
    say to Me:
'These are My children, beloved of Me; I will listen to and
    answer them until they come into the kingdom I have
    prepared for them.'

It can readily be seen that this prophecy is in two parts, the first seven lines describing all the elements of worship which should be evident in every orthodox traditional Charismatic Renewal prayer meeting. Should a prayer meeting not include each of these elements of worship then it cannot be truly in the Spirit of Renewal.

The second part of the prophecy emphasises that it is not necessary nor indeed desirable to add any other type of prayer, novena, or other form of spirituality be it old or new, to the seven-fold way of Charismatic Renewal worship. Sadly a few people tend to arrive regularly with hidden agendas at Charismatic Renewal prayer meetings, resulting in many Renewal groups being led away from their traditional seven-fold way of worship. When this happens then, not surprisingly, the first casualty is the power to heal – it disappears and it vanishes all interest in healing too. It behoves that the core group in every Charismatic Renewal prayer meeting then be constantly on their guard to maintain the traditional seven-fold way of worship. Basically the prophecy set out above confirms that view. I am satisfied that should core groups fail to protect their specific vocation then the Church and indeed the whole world will be the poorer. When Charismatic Renewal prayer meetings and conferences are faithful to their calling, blessings and healings in profusion will be evident, as indicated plainly in the second part of the prophecy under discussion. By the power of the Holy Spirit may this be so *ad multos annos*.

Finally, it needs to be stated emphatically over and over again that the Charismatic Renewal movement is the visible contemplative prayer wing of the Church in the modern world, composed of the people of God who seek to develop a community prayer life on a part time permanent basis as distinct from the contemplative orders of the Holy Church whose members dedicate their entire lives to their vocation. Therefore, the Charismatic Renewal movement does nothing – nothing at all, but astonishingly it never fails to attract those who wish to manipulate it and put it to work. Such people fail utterly to understand the role of Renewal and cannot appreciate that, other than healings of every kind, Charismatic Renewal is not in the business of producing visible results. In the Gospels, we read of Jesus Christ during His public life constantly entreating his disciples, 'to come away and pray a while'. Charismatic Renewal answers that call. May those who seek to change the thrust of Renewal 'back off', and by God's grace enter Renewal, accept it as it is, and enjoy the satisfaction of helping to write Acts 29, while rejoicing in the excitement of being part of the second Pentecost.

IN CONVERSATION, WHEN THE topic of religion arises, Jim, a friend of mine, is wont to declare that he is a Jewish Christian of the Catholic variety, a classification which causes eyebrows to be raised. Quickly he proves the validity of this definition by firstly restating the age-old truth that Christianity springs from Judaism. After all, Jesus Christ was a Jew, as was His mother Mary, His foster-father Joseph and the Apostles too. St Paul, the greatest organiser of the Christian faith, was a Pharisee. Secondly, Jim, emphasising that as Christians are sadly split into many denominations since the Reformation in the west and the breakaway of the seven orthodox Churches in the east, undeniable historical facts, such background explains his declaration of being a Christian of the Catholic persuasion. Inevitably Jim's assertion provokes the comment that history is boring, an observation he counters by warning people to ignore history at their peril, with such an attitude invariably leading to the same mistakes being made which resulted in untold sufferings for past generations. Therefore it behoves reflective Christians to be at least aware of their origin and background which, without any doubt is found primarily in Scripture where it is plainly evident that prophecy abounds.

Now it is well-known that prophecy is, of course, one of the seven elements of worship promoted in the Charismatic Renewal movement. Frankly, I found great difficulty in understanding the function and role of prophecy at Renewal prayer meetings, possibly because I had never previously encountered it at any traditional Catholic service or gathering. However, as seems par for the course for me in this mysterious Charismatic Renewal experience, events directly relating to prophecy were about to overtake me, with startling rapidity too.

The action began at one of the usual Charismatic prayer meetings in 'Avila', Carmelite Monastery, Dublin, in early spring 1993 when the customary silence following the praising of God in tongues was broken by the prophecy, 'I will provide'; it was delivered in confident tones too. It was instantly greeted by exclamations of 'Praise God', 'Thanks be to God', indicating that many there were consoled and encouraged by it. Strangely some time later I received a letter from a man announcing that a very pressing burden caused by debt had now vanished when he unexpectedly found himself in a position to clear all his debts. Apparently, when he had asked me for prayer for that situation I had mentioned the prophecy, 'I will provide'; now he had been delivered from the crucifixion of debt.

Strangely the very next morning after receiving that letter I found myself in Dublin's city centre as I had business calls there. When I had completed these chores I dropped into a cafe for morning coffee and was immediately hailed to a table by George, a friend of mine who was with his mother-in-law. George is a complicated man (aren't we all?) and although deeply interested in the power to heal displayed at Charismatic Renewal meetings, shows no inclination at all to become involved in this movement, deciding to remain on the fringes of it despite many extraordinary experiences. For instance, some months previously, a friend of his had a sixteen year-old daughter stricken with anorexia nervosa. The poor girl lost weight rapidly, was unable to concentrate on her studies and consequently her attendance at school became very spasmodic. Sadly, after months of medical treatment, there was no improvement in her condition either. George then encouraged the frantic mother to become involved in the Charismatic Renewal movement and eventually mother and daughter arrived at 'Avila'. There, after one session of prayer, this girl was instantly cured, her normal appetite returned to her, as did her former enthusiasm for study.

Another unexplainable characteristic of George from my point of view is his refusal to seek anything for himself through prayer. In no way can I identify such an attitude with the Christian faith, as, after all, Jesus Christ specifically stressed that his followers should confidently ask Almighty God, in His name, to grant their needs. Why, even in the prayer given by the Lord, we find five of the seven petitions plainly indicating that not alone should believers ask for favours but should do so positively. But then I suppose in the Father's house there are many mansions.

However that morning in the cafe George exuded happiness and opened the conversation by asking, 'Any good news from the Lord lately Andy?' Responding, I began to tell George and his mother-in-law of the prophecy, 'I will provide', and its remarkable confirmation in the letter I had received, but was stopped in my tracks from expanding on this story when I witnessed the effect that it was having on these two people. Amazingly, George's eyes filled with tears, while his mother-in-law began to cry openly. Sensing the confusion, George broke the silence, explaining, 'Andy, as you know, I run my own business, but after a succession of disastrous deals, last week for the first time in my business life, I found myself broke, down on my uppers.' Next, George went on to describe how the previous day, he was in the city centre with all the money he possessed in his pocket, two single pounds, when out of the blue he bumped into a man he hadn't met for years. Instantly this man exclaimed, 'Good God George, you look ashen! What's the matter?' With this sudden confrontation, George was too overcome to speak, whereupon his long lost friend steered him into a nearby cafe where over coffee George revealed the full extent of his financial position. Haltingly, George told of the collapse of his business, how his bank refused to advance him any further funds, had withdrawn his cheque book and credit cards while seeking an immediate substantial payment towards the reduction of the huge overdraft. Failure to do so on George's part would result in the bank seeking a judgment against him in court, thereby effectively destroying his credibility to trade in the future. This doom and gloom tirade ended with George advancing the view that the only viable alternative open to him was to sell his home, a proposition which frightened the living daylights out of him.

The man opposite remained silent for some minutes, and then he suddenly grabbed George by the arm, ignored the two untouched cups of coffee and walked him purposefully out into the daylight. Next he asked George, 'Where have you your overdraft?' and, on learning the name of the bank, walked George to the nearest branch. There, they met an assistant manager to whom, at his friend's authoritative request, George disclosed his account number and asked for confirmation of the exact amount of his overdraft. Within minutes, with the aid of modern technology, this figure was supplied on a print-out with both men conscious that interest was being added to this sum on a daily basis. George's companion also noted that the considerable sum shown was exactly as disclosed minutes previously in the cafe. After a long perusal of the figures in front of him, the man at George's side swiftly produced his cheque book, wrote a cheque for the full due sum, pushed it across the counter, saying, with quiet authority, 'Ring my bank and confirm that there are sufficient funds available to meet this'. Again within minutes, the cheque was cleared, a lodgement docket was filled out and the whole business transaction was completed when the assistant manager handed the stamped and signed counterfoil to George.

They left the bank with George speechless, and they shook hands on the sunlit pavement as George's benefactor simply remarked, 'There's a fresh start for you. It is a gift, with no strings attached, but there won't be a repeat performance'.

Finally, he said, 'Good luck, George', and was gone, leaving a dumbfounded man standing still gazing at a bank lodgement docket in his hand. At this stage of George's riveting story, when I didn't know whether or not I was listening to fact or fiction, George's mother-in-law dried her tears, and quietly confided, 'Andy, as truly George is married to my daughter, I can vouch for the genuineness of every detail of that story.'

Driving home after that remarkable encounter, I clearly saw the direct connection of the prophecy, 'I will provide', with George's experience which was startlingly similar to the news disclosed in the letter I had received on the previous morning. This double confirmation gave me a deeper insight and an entirely new conception of the function and role of prophecy in Charismatic Renewal. I saw prophecy was much more than just a few comforting words to dwell on for a moment before dismissing them. The prophecy, 'I will provide', is so clearly rooted in Scripture that when I heard it, I instantly associated it with the Word of the Lord, 'I have come to set you free'. Consequently that prophecy is a Word from the Lord, an invitation to His people to apply it to situations of chaos and suffering. Christians should not be surprised. The Word of God was creative in the beginning, is creative now and forever will be creative. But believe me, to actually witness the creative power of the Word in action in life's various situations, is truly a marvellous experience.

JAMES IS AN ENTREPRENEUR who would be described by the media in modern economic jargon as a 'mover and shaker'; he always had ambition to establish and control his own business, and eventually did, after one or more abortive attempts. Now, however, he was up and running, his company expanding in direct proportion to the considerable time and energy he devoted to it. James also found space to praise God in the Charismatic Renewal movement and any time I met him socially, he invariably encouraged me to continue my recording of healings that I witness, constantly referring to these in biblical terms as 'tidings of great joy'.

James' business was primarily a selling organisation

where he had many competitors as one would expect. In the world of commerce and industry, as in every other human activity, one meets the good, the bad and the ugly, and eventually James clashed with a rival firm that he would not classify as good. Understandably the other group held similar views on James' company! This dispute deepened with 'head-to-head' confrontations with the principals of both firms, followed by an exchange of letters and even involving customers, the saga leading in the long run to each side consulting their solicitors. Settlement proved to be still elusive, unfortunately, so the matter was referred to the court. Entering the courts, James was immediately intimidated by his surroundings, enduring very recognisable stress, an experience common to all except the legal profession and court workers. Even people in the public gallery of a court admit to sensing stress in this threatening environment. Although it was a civil case, James could also well identify with the validity of the observation of the solicitor friend of mine that a day in court is certainly no picnic.

With the two opposing parties and their legal teams gathered in the court foyer, an eleventh hour attempt was made to reach an amicable settlement but not a sign of a breakthrough was visible as the hour approached when the case was due to be called. At that precise stage, James withdrew from this legal huddle, overpowered with an overwhelming desire to be rid of all this non-productive hassle, and after a moment's reflection, quickly quit the court precincts and once outside the door, ran to his car. There, he grabbed his car phone and rang me; fortunately I was at home. 'Thank God I got you', James blurted out, obviously very tense. Next he quickly outlined the circumstances of his situation, adding, 'The case is completely deadlocked. In no way do I wish to be in this horrible place. Andy, I just want to be back at my business, doing my job! Please ask the Lord to solve this puzzle. I have only minutes to talk to you.' Appreciating the urgency of the moment, straight away I started praising God, acknowledging that He is not a God of chaos, confusion or disorder, but rather a God of peace, order and tranquillity, while asking that an equitable and just solution be found in this case, quickly. I concluded by advising James to let the Lord into the court foyer before him when he returned. 'Thanks Andy', James replied and the call ended.

How strange it was that I happened to be there to receive his call; I had only returned moments beforehand. I also sincerely hoped that James would follow my advice to let the Lord into the court before him. Although this approach worked very powerfully for me in my business life, I was mystified as to why so many readers of my first book, world-wide, who, identifying with it, reported startling results when acting on this advice. Where did the power come from, I wondered? Tearing asunder this conundrum I was strangely led to confront once again the riddle of the universe of all things. While conscious of the adherents of the many theories on creation ranging from evolution to the 'Big Bang', as a Christian I accept and believe primarily that the Word of God was the first cause of creation. Therefore, I searched the Scriptures to see did the Lord go before any successful human action and I rejoiced when I 'discovered', in the Second Book of Samuel chapter 5, verse 24, why the advice I offered James was so awesomely powerful. It could not be plainer; it was based on the Word of God and that Word is creative! Look it up for yourself.

That same evening, James rang me again; his message was short and clear. 'Andy, you asked me to let the Lord into the court before me. I did so, when I rejoined the pre-court conference. Within half an hour and against all the odds, agreement was reached, the case was withdrawn from the court by the consent of both parties and I was back at work immediately after lunch! Thanks for the prayers, Andy,' he concluded.

TERROR AND FAMILY DISRUPTION caused by drunken hooligan-type behaviour in their home by Pat, the eldest of a family of five, became a regular experience for his parents Richard and Kathleen. Pat left home at nineteen, went to college, secured his degree and immediately was appointed to a good position in industry in Dublin, avoiding emigration which was the lot of most of his class. He rented an apartment and kept in touch with his family who lived in a small town some 30 miles from

135

the city. Pat lived a normal life and was a problem to no one until a girl moved in to live with him. Having no matrimonial ambitions, such 'shacking up' arrangement was mutually acceptable, thus qualifying this pair to be classified by their peers as a truly modern, liberated couple. They became an 'item' around Dublin's bar, club and disco scene, where Pat soon found his vocation in heavy drinking. Not alone did he become fond of drink, he actually appeared to attack it. Pat's 'live-in' girlfriend, a native of the south-west coast of Ireland, spent her Easter, summer and Christmas vacations with her parents, doing likewise at Bank Holiday weekends. Consequently, Pat was alone in his city apartment on these occasions. Therefore, in the spirit of, 'if you can't beat them, join them', Pat was led to return home to his parents too. Naturally he was made very welcome and although his Catholic, God-fearing family couldn't support his bohemian non-Christian lifestyle, they kept communication lovingly open with him. The fact that Pat had put the faith of his fathers 'on hold', describing himself as a non-practising Catholic, hurt his loved ones more than he ever realised.

Not alone did he lose his faith and sobriety, he lost all sense of discretion and sensitivity also. Pat's family were appalled at his drinking sessions on these festive times and very quickly began to dread his homecoming, with his very presence guaranteed to bring trouble galore. On these holiday weekends, Pat would appear in his home town early on Friday and without reporting to the family, would go straight 'on the town', eventually tearing down their door in the early hours of the Saturday morning, roaring to be admitted. There in the sitting-room he would then commence a rowdy, drunken sing-song session, making sleep impossible for everyone in the house, while causing the family acute embarrassment as their neighbours too were disturbed by this riotous lager-lout act. Rising late on the Saturday afternoon, Pat would follow the same routine for the remainder of the weekend. He just became impossible, would not listen to reason and caused so much stress that his parents, Richard and Kathleen, were unable to cope with the problem.

As if things were not bad enough, Christmas seemed to bring out the very worst in him, so in October 1992, Richard and Kathleen, dreading the coming of the season of goodwill, were compelled to seek counselling from a family therapist of Christian persuasion. Quickly they outlined their problem to this professional lady, who could sense that they were terrorised as she heard how, in the previous year, their agony peaked when Pat seriously disrupted their late afternoon family Christmas dinner with an appalling torrent of non-stop abuse. It seemed to Richard, Kathleen and family that Pat's totally unprovoked and unjustified verbal attack was his way of working off his massive hangover while finding unnatural pleasure in ridiculing and pouring scorn on their faith and practices. Almost instantly the counsellor identified their problem, realising Richard and Kathleen's adherence to the obligation to forgive their enemies, 'until 70 times 7', had led them into a cul-de-sac. They could see no escape route. Their counsellor explained that Christianity must always reflect the Natural Law and enshrined in that law were checks and balances of rights and duties. In plain language she explained, whereas Pat as a son had a right to visit his parental home, he had the duty to behave in a reasonable manner when there, such duty running parallel with this right,

Richard and Kathleen were learning that there were two sides to everything. Side by side with that principle was that justice always takes precedence over love, never the reverse. Expanding on this startling news for her clients, their mentor recalled the words from Scripture where Jesus Christ confirmed this truth with His warning, 'What does it profit a man or woman should they gain the whole world and suffer the loss of their eternal souls'. Therefore, the Christian's foremost obligation is to himself and herself, next to one's spouse, then to one's offspring, extending to parents and so on. Proceeding, the counsellor outlined to this husband and wife that it was their duty to ensure that good order and peace prevailed in their home, so that their clan should enjoy the security of family life, which is the unit group of society. Automatically it followed, she maintained, that Pat's attack on them was actually

137

an attack on society itself, warning that should the institution of the family be destroyed, then people would tear each other asunder like wild dogs. Warming to her task, she explained that all human beings, be they Christian or whatever, had the right to defend themselves as best they can against attack. Therefore, as Pat's behaviour was a serious and ongoing assault on their home, not alone had they the right to defend themselves but they had the duty to do so, even basing her submission on the Gospel itself. Unhesitatingly, she drew her attention to what happened when Jesus Christ saw the Temple degraded by commercial activity; He violently ejected both buyers and sellers, denouncing them for turning His Father's House into a den of thieves, whereas it was intended to be a house of prayer where sacrifice was offered to God. For sure, she added, Jesus Christ knew how to keep order in His Father's House! Similarly, while not advocating Richard and Kathleen take violent physical action, she recommended stern, corrective, positive and no-nonsense measures be immediately put in place.

Next, their counsellor suggested that the parents immediately contact their troublesome son, by personal call, telephone or letter, recall to him the hurt he was inflicting by his behaviour pattern, especially over the Christmas holidays the previous year and remind him, as this unacceptable behaviour had continued even during the recent October Bank Holiday, that he was no longer welcome in the family home from that moment onwards. Furthermore, they should demand an instant assurance from Pat that he would cease forthwith calling at their home, adding that should he refuse to give such an unequivocal undertaking, they would consult a solicitor and institute court proceedings to obtain a barring order against him. Initially, Richard and Kathleen were stunned at this revelation, but they were comforted to be released from the stone wall that they faced. In a nutshell, their counsellor had emphasised that in justice no person, Christian or otherwise, had any right to walk all over others. These two harassed parents left their counsellor's presence with a load lifted from their shoulders.

Fired-up with a new appreciation of their problem, Richard and Kathleen did not hang about but that very same day, drafted a letter to their eldest son on the lines indicated by their counsellor. They confirmed that while their deep love for him would never cease or diminish, they had made a firm decision to exclude him from the family home. Convinced that he was unable to handle drink, they assured Pat that their resolution would only change when he opted for total sobriety, adding that a period of twelve months of drink-free behaviour would have to elapse before he would be welcome home again. Having done so, they felt comfortable and at peace with their decision.

Surprisingly, some ten days before Christmas, Pat wrote to his parents, and acknowledged their letter. He accepted their decision without question, astonishingly disclosed that he was now sober for the past month, not having touched a drink, and he explained that he had made other arrangements for his Christmas holidays. As if this was not enough, amazingly Pat enclosed a cheque for a substantial sum to his parents, to wish them a Happy Christmas!

With their three previous Christmas celebrations transformed into hell on earth experiences, the commemoration of the birth of Jesus Christ in 1993 was Heaven itself for Richard, Kathleen and family, with terror-spreading conduct guaranteed to frighten the wits out of this quiet-living, reserved clan, disappearing as quick as a wink. The serenity, tranquillity, joy, relaxation and peace of the feast seemed almost unreal to them, while they could now look forward with hope to a reconciliation with their eldest son, some time in the future, when his cross of drink would have similarly vanished.

Richard and Kathleen are long time friends of mine, so it was very moving indeed for me to listen to their story. Examining the whole affair objectively, the most evident feature of it was finding themselves in a crisis situation beyond their ability to comprehend or solve, these two people refused to surrender to self-pity or inactivity, but instead sought professional assistance which brought them deliverance almost instantly. Maybe there is more truth than poetry in the old adage, 'God helps those who help themselves, but God help those who don't!'

It is important to understand also that Richard and Kathleen's action is a direct contradiction of the 'do nothing but offer it up to the Lord' philosophy, with their stunning result a re-affirmation of positive old-age Christianity in action, based on the advice, 'Pray, knowing everything depends on God, but act as if everything depends on oneself'. When it is fully understood and acted out, it is possible to have the best of both worlds. Christians should not be content with anything less. So many Christians need to hear again and again the consoling prophecy familiar to those who attend Charismatic Renewal prayer meetings, 'Where there is no solution, I will create a solution'. It cannot be any other way when one realises that Gospel is Old English for Good News. I often wonder why the term Good News was dropped for the word Gospel. Strange too that Christians need to be told over and over again that one of the first gifts of the Holy Spirit to them is intelligence. Without doubt it should be used in every situation.

DURING A STAY IN a hotel in the south of Ireland, I happened to meet a man in the coffee shop there, where he was unwinding at the end of a business conference and we quickly struck up a conversation. He was middle-aged, a foreigner who rejoiced in the name of Josef and was 20 years resident in Ireland. When I enquired how he came to settle in Ireland, a strange tale unfolded. The first decade of his life after he finished his degree in his native land was an unmitigated disaster due to alcoholism, he disclosed. His story was gripping to listen to, as he revealed how, on waking out of a drunken coma in hospital, he found his bewildered parents, at his bedside, gazing down at him. Josef described his self-disgust and humiliation at that moment as the most horrifying experience of his life, when, at a loss for words, he cried out as innocently as a child, 'When did all this drinking begin, Mum?' He continued, 'My God, and you can imagine how these two gentle people must have felt, considering that I had crucified them by my conduct over so many years!' It was a month before he was 'dried-out' and in fit condition to return to work, but when he did so, he had a gut feeling that his days in that organisation were numbered. Out of the blue then, he heard of a job opportunity in Ireland, applied for the position, was interviewed, and more to his surprise, was successful. His God-fearing parents were overjoyed at the news, with his Mum remarking, 'Thanks be to God. Surely there must be very few, if any, on that little holy island who would be interested in drinking!'

Josef flew into Shannon Airport and was met in the arrivals hall by a representative of the firm who had hired him, when to his utter amazement the first words the man heard in Ireland were, 'What will you have to drink?' It was the beginning of many surprises for Josef in his new environment, for he had hardly settled into the job when he met an Irish girl and was shocked beyond belief when he fell in love. Women had never previously figured on Josef's agenda, as after business hours, his alcohol based tunnel vision outlawed everything except the end of a glass. Cold stone sober since he had left mainland Europe, Josef lived with a constant, almost overpowering desire to give the two finger salute to life and surrender to the booze but realised that should he do so, his appointment would be summarily terminated at the end of his six-month mandatory probation period. He was so stressed that he unburdened himself to his newly-found female companion, amazed to hear himself declare that he was drawn to do so as he hoped some day to ask her for her hand in marriage. Learning of his formidable track record in the alcohol stakes, very sensibly she pointed him towards Alcoholics Anonymous, while telling him in no uncertain terms that she wouldn't even consider a serious relationship until he had completed a two-year drink free period. Very strangely at this stage of our conversation, he revealed that he had now no difficulty in accepting the doctrine of Hell, as to use his own words, 'I have been there and back!' But how proud he was, recalling that special time some fifteen years previously, when suddenly all desire to drink vanished, leaving him free to develop a highly successful career as well as marrying the love of his life. As Josef and I strolled out of the coffee shop, he said,

'Thanks for listening to me, Andy', and was gone.

It was a typical 'ships that pass in the night' meeting, as our paths never crossed again. Josef's story emphasised the truth of the assertion that the difference between a glitteringly successful career and the plight of a 'wino' sleeping rough in a cardboard box, is thinner than silk thread.

Kevin, whom I met in Africa, would have been more than interested in Josef's story, I realised too. This man easily stood out in a crowd, was blond, carried himself as straight as a whip at 6 feet 2 inches, weighed in at $15^{1}/_{2}$ stones and was very well built. A fitness fanatic, it would be no surprise either if his body fat registered a nil figure. The love of his life was rugby and as he made progress through to the first team of his club and seemed destined for representative honours, he quickly found that he had a problem – off the field. While Kevin had no bother meeting and mixing with people, the rowdy sing-song, all male sessions which invariably follow the traditional after-match dinner never failed to fill him with dread, with his shyness precluding him participating. How he envied people who could stand up at these functions, tell bawdy yarns, render raucous songs, do impersonations or whatever. Seeing him so ill at ease on these occasions, one of his club mates, Tom, suggested that he take a pint or two after dinner. 'It will banish your shyness, Kevin,' Tom forecast. Kevin, 20 years of age and teetotal, took the proffered advice and it certainly worked, putting his shyness to flight as Tom foretold. However, twelve months to the day when he was first introduced to the mood altering drug alcohol, Kevin found himself naked in a padded cell of a psychiatric hospital; he had a massive drink problem!

When his sanity returned, he was released from the secure hospital wing and settled in a ward where he met his fellow patients, all sharing a common complaint. He underwent counselling, group in-patient therapy, and family therapy which included close friends, the whole drying out experience frightening him almost to despair. Kevin restlessly walked the corridors of the hospital, alone, between these sessions, endeavouring to come to terms with this utterly unexpected development in his life, and while doing so, one evening heard sounds of music and song coming from one of the lecture halls. He paused outside the entrance and, seeing a man who was obviously a non-patient about to enter, enquired, 'What's going on in there?' In reply, this man held the door open for Kevin, stood back and replied, 'Come on in and see for yourself'. Kevin entered, sat down, listening and looking in wonder – he had inadvertently stumbled into his first Charismatic Renewal prayer meeting.

One hour later he left that lecture hall knowing that it was love at first sight, and he returned to the ward with his confidence restored, knowing his days there were numbered. He rang home and his parents were astonished to hear how self-assured he sounded, and he made their day when he announced that he hoped to be discharged within days, although he had no official confirmation whatsoever of this news. Kevin put down the phone, went in search of the night sister, who, having listened to his story, observed, 'You have contracted gate fever!' Actually, she knew immediately he approached her that he was cured, but whether or not it would be the first of many admissions in the future for him, she or nobody could tell.

Twenty years later, I heard Kevin's story as we chatted together at a Charismatic Renewal meeting that I attended in Africa, where I learned that Kevin just walked away from his alcohol problem on his discharge from hospital. Laughingly, he observed, 'They got no repeat business from me, Andy!' He struck it rich in business, and was happily married, while deeply involved in Renewal. He also headed up a voluntary organisation assisting young people who, although technically qualified and wishing to go into business on their own, were short of start-up capital. It was, he said, his way of honouring the Lord's new commandment and also in thanksgiving for having been given a second chance in life. Movingly, Kevin often confessed that he could well identify with those in prison cells on death row after his experience at gazing at skid row when he found himself so quickly locked into alcohol.

I was vividly reminded of Josef's and Kevin's brush with alcoholism when Tony phoned me. He identified himself and having read my books sought an appointment. Laughingly, I responded that I did not receive people at my home, for should I attempt to do so, my house would resemble an outdoor department of a hospital. Furthermore, I told him that I did not hold clinics either nor accept money for my services in the healing ministry of the Holy Church. 'How do you manage then?' he enquired, incredulously. Before replying, I asked what was bothering him and then heard the story of his eldest daughter Joan, a married lady with two children, living in London. Her husband Alex was doing well, and she loved their life in the fast lane, but problems were signalled loud and clear when she began to drink to excess. Alex's job called for him to socialise and project the public image of his firm by gracing formal business occasions with his presence. A confident, serene partner at his side was essential to reinforce the whole PR package designed by his board of directors. Sadly, though, Joan's behaviour at what should have been her shining hour began to hinder and embarrass Alex, making it imperative for him to confront her and draw a line in the sand. He did so and in an effort to pull herself together, Joan arrived in Dublin for a short holiday and unburdened herself to her parents, fearful that her marriage might collapse. Now here was Tony, her father, seeking any assistance I could give. Responding, I pointed him, his spouse and Joan to Renewal, recommended that they read daily from St John's Gospel, chapter 2, 'The wedding at Cana in Galilee' for her healing and the call ended with a short, shared prayer.

At the end of the very next meeting at 'Avila' after his call, Tony approached me. He had Joan with him. They introduced themselves, explained that they had travelled a journey of two hours to get to the meeting and sought prayer for Joan's healing. Not alone was fear plainly visible in her expression, but she also projected the image of a woman being hunted and harried. Having had an outline of Joan's problem from her Dad's phone call, when I gently mentioned that prayer in tongues was considered very efficacious in the presence of alcoholism, I noticed that she was neither surprised nor offended by the use of the term. If anything, it seemed to totally concentrate her mind as she blurted out, 'Oh, Mr O'Neill, I'm terrified of losing my husband, home and children because of my anti-social behaviour'. Quietly, I explained to them, in the presence of difficulties where there seems to be no natural explanation (excessive drinking in her case) there may be a supernatural explanation – of the wrong order. I repeated that many of those active in the Healing Ministry avow that praying in tongues is the only effective method of combating alcoholism. Tongues, I explained, are inexplicable too, but hopefully the Holy Spirit takes these sounds, translates them into words meaningful in a particular situation and gives them to Jesus who presents them to the Father. More importantly, I pointed out, that it is also consoling to remember that prayer to Our Heavenly Father, through His only begotten Son Jesus Christ by the power of the Holy Spirit, is unreservedly recommended by Vatican II in its document on prayer. Next, with her consent, I began with another, the formal custom of the laying on of hands, a tradition which even pre-dates Christianity itself, and asked Joan's Dad to join me too, before quietly praying in tongues. With the number seeking prayer in 'Avila' dictating that the time spent with each person be strictly limited, our four person huddle of intercession must have finished in under three minutes or so. This short duration practice is traditionally Scriptural too according to St Matthew's Gospel, chapter 10, verses 1–3, a reading which confirms the awesome economy of time, action and word displayed when Jesus Christ healed. We wished them well, they thanked us and left, with Joan walking into a future which seemed very uncertain indeed, not alone for her, but for her spouse, children and extended family.

Some three months later, Joan's Dad, Tony, wrote to me. Apparently, the brief stay in Ireland with her parents, the reading of my books and the 'Avila' experience had administered to her a sharp shock, resulting in her resolve to finish totally with alcohol, a decision she took within days of arriving back at her home in London. She even rang her parents, telling them that she had subsequently attended three glittering social functions with her high-flying husband Alex, did not touch a drop

145

of drink nor had she any inclination to do so and actually drove her husband home from these gatherings, to his utter amazement. The husband and wife show, as far as his firm was concerned, was certainly back on the road. Truly, it's an ill-wind that blows nobody any good, with Alex delighted that he could now enjoy a few drinks in comfort with his ever-present police check worry a thing of the past. How proud Tony was to be reporting in his letter to me that his daughter also sailed blissfully though the flash points of Christmas and New Year celebrations without a care in the world.

Tony recalled also in his letter that when praying with his daughter, Joan, I reminded her of her seventeenth birthday, when she was on the threshold of life, foot loose, fancy free, on the 'look out', without a care in the world, while brimful of energy and joy. Although I don't recall it, seemingly I finished the prayer saying, 'Joan – you saw that day. May you see it again!' Finally Tony praised God in his letter. I suppose one should not be surprised when spontaneous prayer is answered down to the last detail as Scripture promises when people are asked to speak in the Lord's name, they should not worry because He guarantees to put His words into their mouths. Whatever any one else may think, Joan's parents are fully convinced that they have witnessed a miracle when they view the radically changed lifestyle of their daughter.

I hope that Joan may link her deliverance from alcoholism to the grace of the Holy Spirit, come to discover the most powerful prayer of all for Christians is based on and rooted in the Word, confirmed in Corinthians chapter 4, verse 20 which affirms that the kingdom of God is not just words, it is power. My wish is that Joan might meet the Lord Jesus Christ through the Charismatic Renewal prayer movement, where she will also learn in I Timothy chapter 4, verse 8 that spirituality is effective not alone in her present life (which power she has already seen) but more importantly promises eternal happiness in the next life, to where all are heading, even those who do not believe.

IT WAS VERY LATE on a Friday afternoon again as John, home

John instantly appeared in the kitchen, heated the milk for the wheat flakes, made the tea, served her in respectful silence and withdrew. Ten years had elapsed since he last performed these rites. The arrival of her twelve year-old twin daughters and John junior shattered the calm, however, with her son in confusion asking, 'What is Dad doing in the garden?' His Mum replied, 'Eat your breakfast first and then go and check for yourself', as his sisters looked knowingly at each other. Apparently the gift of intuition comes earlier to the female of the species. John junior swallowed his breakfast in record time and scampered to the front garden, while Margaret, leaving the girls to clear away the breakfast things, wandered towards the front door, the early morning sunshine heralding a glorious spring day. She was not though in any way prepared for the sight which met her as she viewed her car, all four doors and boot open, car mats scattered on the driveway, as the two men in her life chatted, as they beavered away, valeting it!

Margaret retreated upstairs and was finishing dressing when she received the news that her husband had arranged to drive the children to their music and tennis lessons! Leaving her room, she saw John's bedroom door ajar, with windows wide open airing it. Standing dead still on the landing, she attempted to come to terms with her surroundings. The normal Saturday morning scene saw her driving the children, while John's bedroom door would be shut as he lay in a drunken slumber, rising in mid-afternoon, to head to his local for pub grub, returning home after midnight.

Being alone on a Saturday morning, sitting in a deck chair soaking up the sun was a new situation for Margaret and having only birds and bees to keep her company, it would be only natural that she should indulge in the luxury of taking stock of her position. Perhaps, like many women in her circumstances, influenced by the world-wide feminist movement, she might accept that her marriage was long since over on the grounds that where there is no conjugal love, there is no marriage. She could very well also conclude that her husband's total disinterestedness in counselling in any shape or form, while holding in derision the aims and philosophy of movements such as

Alcoholics Anonymous, was further proof, if needed, that their union was no longer in existence. Leaving her to rear three children single-handedly, and showing no interest in their health, schooling or future other than supplying more than adequate funds for these purposes, signalled John's decision to opt for the single lifestyle, unencumbered by dependents. Margaret would surely be aware too that while the obligation of forgiveness is at the very heart of Christianity, it did not give the right to one partner to make a doormat of the other. In relationships, as in everything else, justice must always come before love; the reversal would make the practice of Christianity philosophically impossible, bringing with it widespread terror, chaos and disorder. As she sat and mused, Margaret, possessing a professional qualification, might well have decided to leave her spouse on the very first day that their last child left home and so begin a new life for herself, an option exercised by many women in her position nowadays. These various alternatives to other feasible propositions could well have been reviewed by her.

Her husband too, as he busied himself attending to the social needs of his family on that Saturday morning, must also have been conscious of the possibility that his inexcusable behaviour of the past decade might well have mortally wounded his marriage. Therefore, whether or not they could ever come together again, nobody could know, but John must have known, now in his sober senses, that he had a mountain to climb, and the challenge could well be beyond him, unless he received help. From whom? From what quarter? Obviously, sobriety brings its own problems, with bewildering swiftness to alcoholics in the 'dried drunk' state. Quite a new scene for a person who boasted of being liberated, needing neither God, man, woman nor child.

I never knew that John and his clan were on the face of God's earth until contacted by an interested third party. Later, one of the two main characters in this human drama, John, telephoned me. He was completely cool, calm and collected, giving his name, address and telephone number, and he told his story in a very telegrammatic manner, beginning by describing his never-to-be-forgotten weekend six months previously when he inadvertently picked up one of my books. He was seemingly dumbfounded on the one hand, as from the moment he finished reading it in the early hours of that Saturday morning, he never had the slightest inclination or desire to take another alcoholic drink, irrespective of the occasion. On the other hand however, the awful injustice and damage he had inflicted on his family was also instantly borne on him. Whether or not he would ever again be accepted in his home as a husband and father is anybody's guess, but I gathered that following his experience on his memorable weekend, he had concentrated his life on one day at a time, while being physically and mentally present to his wife and children every evening and at weekends. I hope he realises that this philosophy is at the heart of the Alcoholics Anonymous movement and is also one of the ground rules of Christian behaviour being founded on the Word of the Living God. John didn't want a shoulder to cry on, nor did he seek prayer; the only reason for his call was to say a simple 'Thank you' to me for writing my books. He did so very graciously and the phone went down. Despite his typical English 'stiff upper lip' attitude and laid-back, objective approach, I appreciated that I had just spoken to a man who had been delivered from evil.

My books undoubtedly brought him hope, that's for sure, but he will also need the other, theological virtues, faith and love; the three cannot be separated. I trust that John appreciates that his faith will not be renewed unless he practises it, and surely he must also know that tender, loving constant care of his spouse and children, seeking nothing in return, is the only possible behaviour pattern guaranteed to ensure the re-establishment of his role in the family. The happiness of five people and possibly their eternal destiny may well depend on his acceptance of the primacy of the spiritual. Otherwise, all his feverish efforts, being foundationless, are doomed to failure. May John make the right choice.

6

THE PROBLEM OF EVIL

I remember from my student days attending a lecture by a celebrated academic who had the reputation of being one of the
world's leading authorities on company balance sheets. One
quote of his always remained with me: 'Ladies and gentlemen,
whenever you are asked to comment on a balance sheet,
always preface your remarks with the phrase, "It appears that
..."'! Nowadays, the more I study my Christian faith, I am
absolutely convinced that whenever a Christian believer is
asked to comment or make a statement on it, such a person
would be well-advised to use this prefix. Consequently, in
matters of the faith of my fathers, I am completely 'turned off',
many times by preachers, teachers and authors, who tend to
lay down the law in black and white. To me, one of the fundamental principles of Christianity can be summed up in a five
word phrase, almost 2,000 years old – 'The mystery of our
faith'. Apart from Euclid, QED (*Quod Erat Demonstrandum*)
should be used very, very sparingly by Christian philosophers.

Coincidentally after my student days and in my formative
adult years an extremely wise priest friend, the late Fr Tom
Aherne of Waterford, to whom I and so many others owe an
immense debt of gratitude, always advanced the view that
whatever chance one might have of reaching some slight
understanding of the Fall of Adam and Eve, no one has the
slightest idea why or how the angels fell. In that context too,
my late mentor, while accepting that the effects of original sin
– darkness of the understanding, weakness of the will and
inclination to evil – have been ever-present in people since the
dawn of history, the one element in the human species which
suffered most at the Fall of our first parents is, he held, our
intellect or understanding. In other words, if even a finite mind

in an unimpaired state could ever hope to remotely understand, unravel or explain the infinite, what chance then have we of doing so, with minds severely darkened by the effects of the Fall. Even with the last four things for a Christian – death, judgment, Heaven and Hell – only one can be factually defended – death. With the other three, we are in the presence of the deepest mystery.

Such thoughts surfaced recently when I visited a dear friend whose wife, a chronic invalid, has suffered grievously for over a decade. During the visit, my friend invited me to lay hands on his beloved for healing. This lovely Catholic lady, faithful wife and mother, reacted instantly, blurting out, 'I don't want to hear about God! Why has He left me in this mess, paralysed, utterly dependent on others for everything, whilst in indescribable pain, despite the constant pleas of so many of His faithful?' Then she broke down uncontrollably. I had no answer. Of course, I know that St Paul taught that the sufferings of 1,000 lifetimes is a small price to pay for eternal salvation, but was that a plausible explanation, acceptable to my afflicted friend at that moment, in the depth of her torment? Moreover, how could this helpless woman view the quality of the justice of God, in the short term, which Christians believe is infinite? Again, could she subscribe to the assertion expressed in the Good Book that, 'The Lord is close to the broken-hearted'?

Similarly, I will never forget sitting by the bedside of a dying ten year-old boy. A young priest sat beside me and, looking at the scene, threw up his hands exclaiming, 'Andy, I have no answer'. God bless him for his honesty, but although both of us prayed for the boy's healing, days later, that same priest was one of the celebrants at that innocent child's Requiem Mass. The mother of that gorgeous boy was inconsolable, her Catholic faith bringing her no comfort whatsoever. She refused point blank to contemplate or even consider the possibility of the existence of God or even spirituality of any kind. At the death of her son, her faith vanished. Whether or not she ever regained it, I know not. Similarly, no one can understand why an infinitely loving God summarily calls to judgment a parent

155

of a young family, thereby leaving the surviving spouse and children terror-stricken, broken-hearted and often confused, while deprived in so many ways.

In cases like these, all is darkness for a believer in God, standing before His absolute will. In like manner, chronic invalidism, sometimes lasting a life-time, poses unanswerable questions for Christians too. Believe me, it is deeply disturbing listening to mock atheists, who label such factual happenings as classic examples of black comedy in relation to the existence of God. So you can easily understand in the light of these and many other personal experiences during my twenty years or so in the Healing Ministry of the Holy Church, how appalled I am when I come across simplistic observations like, 'God never tempts us beyond our strength!' Moving from the personal to the world scene in this same vein, I recall too a Catholic man who when confronted by the horror of the Holocaust in the Second World War, on reflection, lost his faith. He asked, 'How could a God who is infinitely just, loving, merciful and good, stand idly by and allow over 6,000,000 of His chosen people, men, women and children, die in gas ovens having endured inhuman degradation, torture and starvation?' The enquirer, on failing to discover adequate answers to this horrible happening, discarded his belief in God, became an atheist, and got on with his life, faithless. The fact that millions of Jews, despite the Holocaust, still fervently believe in the God of Abraham, Isaac and Jacob made no difference to him.

Again on the global scene, the horror of the First World War in Europe was appalling. Similarly the loss of life, awful injuries and widespread death and destruction of both combatants and civilians in the Second World War was a nightmare which came true world-wide. It lasted all of six years, culminating with the unbelievable havoc wrought by the atomic bomb, instantly vapourising cities in Japan, with thousands of their inhabitants, bringing suffering, death and disaster on a scale heretofore unimaginable on this earth.

While on this theme, we can include global natural disasters of drought, violent flooding, mud slides, earthquakes,

hurricanes and the like often described as 'acts of God' in economic life, classified as uninsurable hazards by the insurance
industry. These disasters too bring awful suffering, distress
and death to thousands regularly, with no plausible answers
when questions on the providence of God are asked by objective, faithless people in search of solid evidence for the existence of a Supreme Being. Let's not forget either the ultimate
injustice involved when one person deliberately deprives
another of life, an act so violently unjust that Christians believe
that it cries to Heaven for vengeance. All is not lost though
when people lose their Christian faith when overcome by a
sudden unexplainable loss of a loved one or when surrounded
by horrible events of gigantic proportions. That the Lord God
will certainly make allowances for their reactions, on
Judgement Day, is a conclusion that we must come to, remembering His infinite mercy. No person has any hope in the next
life without it.

What we are painting here is a scenario of darkness, gloom
and doom, which regrettable is not fictional. Therefore, irrespective of whether or not one is theist, atheist, agnostic, secular humanist or indifferent, in this world of ours, there is good
and evil. We know too that it has always been so since the
dawn of history and that the greatest minds have failed to
solve the riddle of the problem of evil. The aim of this casual
study is not in any way to supply the answer to the problem
posed by the presence of evil, all too visible in people and in
the elements surrounding us, but rather to examine how we
can accommodate this problem with the faith professed by
Christians. First, as Christians, we can't walk away from the
effects of evil, some of which we have just listed, and pretend
that our faith solves everything. While followers of Christ believe that He had defeated the power of evil forever in His life,
passion, death, and resurrection and has redeemed the human
race, sickness of mind and body with diseases of all kinds and
description ending with death for all, still remain. Why has it
to be thus? Why was it that some angels and our first parents
fell from the grace of an original, perfect state of existence? Our
explanation, readily offered, is this double disaster and

tragedy happened because our Maker gave free will to those He created. Should this be the only explanation then, in the light of the history of creation over millions of years and its subsequent suffering, impossible to quantify, one has to pose two questions – first, 'Was it all worth while?' and second, 'Was there any other way?' Whether or not the answer to the first question is positive or negative, the fact remains that, 'What you see, you got!'; the present visible world and the condition of those in it is the only existence known to mankind, irrespective of what faith abounds. Also, as the human race is totally and inadequately equipped to deal with why the angels fell, we are compelled to close the book on that subject as it is utterly beyond human comprehension. At least there is some compensation in doing so, as it effectively halves the problem of evil for us!

So, concentrating on the human condition then, personally speaking, the basic and primary satisfaction I have always cherished since I came to the use of reason is the mind-blowing realisation that I am! I am a human being! I am alive! I could have missed out on this experience of being born! So, love it or leave it, I exult in life! I am truly grateful for having been born! Grateful to whom? Naturally to my beloved parents, God rest them, and then right back to our first parents. Grateful? But immediately I accept that I have the capacity to experience feelings and emotions of every conceivable kind, which lifts me supremely above animal life therefore I must conclude that there is an element in my make-up other than mind and body. This intrinsic non-material part of me is classified as the soul and being non-organic, it is quite reasonable to conclude that it is not subject to the natural law governing mind and body. Therefore, it will not be destroyed or end in death. This awesome realisation, added to my delight of life, gives me then immeasurable satisfaction. Now I know that after the death of my body, the 'inner me' will live forever in a personalised spiritual existence. Simplistic reasoning? Maybe so, but it suits me as I can find no other realistic, plausible explanation of the nature of mankind.

The next consideration confronting me in this feeble

attempt to endeavour to arrive at some understanding of the problem of evil is the fact that I am a Christian. A casual glance at my family tree instantly reveals that at least six successive generations of my people were Catholic. Therefore, I was born into the Catholic faith. I didn't deserve, earn or win it. The faith I possess is a free gift to me. From the beginning, I accepted without question, but again on coming to the use of reason, I constantly examined and explored it (an ongoing process in my life), and as I have written previously I find that I get as much and more from my Catholicism as from any other religion, sect or cult. I'm not breaking any new ground either when I profess that the source of my faith is tradition and Scripture. It must be in that order as the infant Church was up and running for most of a century before the first word of the New Testament was written. I believe too that Jesus Christ, true God and true Man by His coming amongst us broke the power of evil forever over mankind. Conversely though, I know that the effects of evil still remain, a fact which troubles me. Sadly, it is indeed self-evident, with suffering and misery being just as intensely universal since the redemption. Why had it to be in this manner?

Discussing the crucifixion of Christ with a Catholic layman deeply steeped in the Word, he advanced the view that Christ had to enter into His passion and death because the human race was in such a fix that there was no other possible way of breaking the power of evil. On reflection, I find no joy in that solution either for should I agree with it I am accepting that God was limited to one option which, besides being a contradiction in terms, is repudiated by the words of the Angel Gabriel at the Annunciation, 'With God, nothing is impossible'. Therefore I must admit that when I probe the problem of evil with my very finite mind I finish up running round in circles, getting exactly nowhere. The best answer I can come up with is that as a Christian, I live by faith, not by fact and that there is no faith without doubt. Irrefutable facts proving conclusively, i) the existence of God, ii) explaining the problem of evil in all aspects, iii) defending totally and entirely the principles of Christianity and iv) solving the riddle of existence, simply do not exist. One of the Fathers of the Church (a woman actually – how unscientific we remain when denied the use of inclusive language!) held that when we die, God will explain all things in the twinkling of an eye, while also demonstrating how He draws good from evil. Until then, seemingly, even those with the brightest intellects must live out life as 'in the glass darkly'. Why even one of the Apostles, Thomas, in the firm knowledge that there was no human witness to the Resurrection, refused point blank to believe that Christ had risen from the dead. Dramatically then when Thomas was confronted by the risen Christ, he professed his total belief, leading Jesus Christ to observe that those who believe without seeing Him (i.e. without proof) are blessed people, no less.

Despite the darkness surrounding these great challenging philosophical and theological questions, Christians must always maintain a lively interest in these adventurous fields of speculation for in no other way can the frontiers of Christian understanding be advanced. One of the great advantages of such activity is that it discourages those who might be tempted to brain-wash or manipulate fellow Christians. Above all, it is vital always to remember that Christians should never be discouraged when stumped by the problem of evil, but should be consoled and encouraged by the Word of the Lord in Jeremiah, chapter 33, verse 3.

So apparently, seeking to solve the problem of evil from the Christian stand-point is as difficult as to play a round of golf alone with a blindfold on! Sickness of mind and body with suffering of every possible kind and description, viewed in the concept of a God who is infinitely loving, kind and merciful, always has been, is, and always will be an unfathomable mystery. Even St Paul is totally unconvincing to me when he writes that in suffering, Christians make up for what was lacking in Christ's ministry on earth. Is he seriously saying that Jesus Christ, the second person of the Most Holy Trinity, true God and true Man, and therefore infinite (i.e. nothing is impossible to Him) failed to complete the task of redemption? Maybe Paul should have left the problem of evil alone. It wasn't the only time that Paul was wide of the mark either as his views of women generally, their status in the Church, and his comments on the relationship between a female and her spouse must be a major embarrassment to the Church today. Events have totally overtaken his teachings on the role of women in this age, as everyone is well aware. Just as in the early centuries, the Church had to soft pedal the traditional, firmly held belief of Christians (including the Apostles and St Paul himself) on the imminence of the second coming of Christ, which didn't happen, it will have to close the book on St Paul's philosophy of women and instead concentrate on his jewels of wisdom and spirituality found in the Acts of the Apostles and in his epistles. After all, despite his shortcomings in the light of how life developed and in the knowledge that he fully expected Christ to return before he (Paul) died, St Paul remains the greatest interpreter of the Christian faith.

The kernel of my argument is that theologians and Scripture scholars will always be vitally necessary for the work of evangelisation because the source of the faith, tradition and Scripture, needs to be constantly studied and revised in the light of new discoveries. It has always been so since the time so long ago when we realised that the sun did not stop still in the heavens as Scripture plainly says. Therefore, those who discourage objective examination of things spiritual even by interested lay people, run the risk of inflicting serious damage to the Church. Jesus Christ said that He came to set the flock free; personal freedom then, with all its attendant risks must never be compromised. Enlightened freedom properly understood with decisions arrived at after frank and free discussions between priest and people is light years apart from 'a la carte Christianity'. The two must never be confused. To my mind one of the worst things that could happen in the Church would be that the flock be discouraged from asking questions, as when the laity lose interest, they may well vote with their feet and walk right out of the Church. In all honesty then, when confronting the problem of evil, there is only one conclusion that I can come to – it remains a total mystery. Believing that all will be revealed on the Last Day, until then Christians should leave God be God and get on with their lives, endeavouring, as best they can, to fulfil the two great commandments, exercising their faith by God's grace in the name of Jesus Christ to the glory of the Father by the power of the Holy Spirit.

It appears (there is that phrase again!) that Christians have little conception of the mystery of suffering in all its forms in relation to the God they believe in but live in hope, looking forward to a perfect, eternal, sorrow-free, personal existence in the next life. Believers can only come to terms with evil in this life by looking forward to the fulfilment of the promise of Jesus Christ that in following His Way, they are laying up treasure for themselves in Heaven where thieves do not break in and steal nor rust or moth decay. It is a hope to non-believers who are condemned to die without hope; but most of those don't give a damn and say that it is no big deal anyway. Allowing for Christianity is a difficult creed to live by, it certainly enshrines the most comforting and consoling prospect imaginable when life draws to an end as it will for believer and non-believer alike. In this respect, I recall attending a Requiem Mass for a mutual friend and on hearing the homily, an atheist colleague with me whispered, 'Where does all this talk about a next life leave me, Andy?' Maybe, despite their brashness, 100% card carrying, fully paid-up atheists may not be all as sure of their ground as we imagine.

A basic hope for Christians is that good will in the long run triumph over evil even though this hope is dismissed by unbelievers and labelled, 'Live horse until you get grass', as they point to the widespread chaos, disorder, suffering and death on this earth as a mockery of God's creation. Christians can only combat such attacks by constantly professing their faith by re-echoing the wondrous shout of triumph first heard 2,000 years ago by an unbelieving world when a former fallen woman, beside herself with joy ran breathlessly from a tomb crying, 'The Lord is Risen!' Jesus Christ had indeed risen from the dead, this Good News even shocking the man destined to become the first Pope with the Apostles non-plussed too on hearing it.

For sure, human beings have not a lasting dwelling here – nobody but nobody is remaining in this world permanently.

No wonder, notwithstanding all its mysteries, the practice of Christianity has been described as enlightened selfishness. I'll drink to that! That's the glory road, the only route on the journey here on earth which leads to the sure realisation of the highest conceivable ambition for people of every age. The achievement of all other possible aims and goals in life at the expense of this pearl of great price spells irretrievable personal disaster. May the Good Lord deliver us and our loved ones from it. To examine the problem of evil through the eyes of an ordinary plain, middle-of-the-road Catholic lay person was one of the reasons which motivated me to write this book. Now I am satisfied that at least I have had a shot at it, as it constantly throws its long shadow over situations where I become involved as the following story will exemplify.

In the early summer of 1994, I received a letter from Sue in the south-west region of Ireland. She had read my three books on healing and was aware that I visit St Vincent's Hospital in Dublin as a member of the Society of St Vincent de Paul. In her letter, Sue very respectfully requested me to visit her brother Tom, who was a patient there and seriously ill. She also acknowledged that she would fully understand should my work load prevent me from doing so. Sue's letter further revealed that her brother was a deaf mute from birth and married to a lady who was similarly handicapped. They had been blessed with three perfectly healthy children, which in itself filled me with awe and with the deepest admiration of them. Days later, when in the hospital, I discovered Tom. He was an isolation nursing case, so I was obliged to seek permission to visit him. The nursing sister in charge, when I introduced myself, immediately confirmed that Tom was expecting me. Next, I gowned up and donned the mandatory rubber gloves, but was informed that I could not take my pocket Scripture with me into his room. Should I do so, it would have to remain in that isolated area from whence it would eventually be taken to the incinerator! I was also instructed to confine my visit to three or four minutes, while learning that our communication would consist of the patient lip-reading me.

When I entered the room, I was aghast at the sight. There

was the patient, dripped and tubed but how that poor shadow of a body sustained life was beyond me. Unquestionably though, his eyes lit up with excitement, hope and expectation when the nurse introduced me by writing on the pad at his bedside locker. Flashing through my mind at that moment were thoughts like, 'How can I possibly identify a God whom I believe is infinitely just, loving and merciful with the pitiable sight before me?' Here was a man so seriously sick, that at one stage of his illness he was only given some 24 hours to live. Now he found himself 100 miles or more from his loved ones, surrounded by doctors, consultants and nurses, all strangers with his communication limited to pen and paper. Instantly accepting my utter inadequacy in this frightfully stressful scene, I asked myself, 'What in Heaven's name Andy are you doing here?' even recalling in a bizarre way a one-line car sticker, 'I'd rather be playing tennis!' Rather than be in the position that I found myself in, maybe I should be lining up a putt with friends on my golf course, so close too, I pondered. Marvelling at the incredible speed at which the human mind can make observations and visualise options, but realising that I was engaged in the visitation of the sick by my own free choice (and by God's grace), I smiled and raised my hand to salute the patient. Without a shadow of a doubt, Tom's reaction to my visit wordlessly indicated that he welcomed me unreservedly. Forming words soundlessly was a new experience for me so I endeavoured to make myself understood in a telegrammatic manner, indicating that I prayed regularly with sick people, seeking their restoration to full health and would do so with him, with his permission. Tom's response was totally positive, his nodding head indicating complete agreement with my proposition.

Keeping it simple, I then asked the Lord to heal Tom by the power of the Word of the Living God, 'Heal the sick', while acknowledging that I never limit His power in any situation, an attitude to prayer of petition that I copied from the Angel Gabriel. Tom vigorously agreed, so much actually that he seemed to be cheering me on! I continued on, sensing that he was getting maybe some 70% of my little message, but, constrained by the time limit on my visit, I asked him to join me in the Lord's prayer. Amazingly then, I discovered that I had no difficulty in lip-reading him so we added the Hail Mary and Gloria. Finally, making the sign of the Cross on his forehead with my gloved hand, I slowly withdrew, waving him farewell, with Tom responding by lifting, ever so slightly, his poor, dripped hand. His smile expressing his thanks was so genuine that it touched me deeply. I returned to the nurse's station, removed my gloves and protective clothing, disinfected my hands as directed, picked up my jacket and Scripture and made my way to the open ward to continue my evening's work, totally confused.

If I were God, I wouldn't leave Tom in the state I found him – not for one instant, but as I have long since come to the conclusion that I am not God I accept situations as I find them. The only aspect of the whole scene which made any sense to me was that I was asked to call on Tom and pray for healing. Having done so, by God's grace, it was consoling to know that my responsibilities ended there. Although everything else that I witnessed in the patient's room was meaningless, senseless and utterly beyond comprehension to me (or to anyone else), the awful truth was that it was a fact of life. Instantly then, in my mind, I placed Tom in the Lord's care, made an act of confidence in God's providence and as a self-preservation technique acquired over the years, detached myself as much as I could from the whole encounter. How comforting it is to know that, in all situations, Jesus Christ is Lord – not me! The ultimate responsibility lies with Him – not with the simple labourer in the vineyard of the sick. In the Healing Ministry in particular it is of paramount importance to know and accept one's status.

That beautiful early summer evening passed, high summer came to Ireland in 1994, sadly only recognisable by reference to the calendar, my sea, sand and sunless Irish holiday came and went and autumn arrived, bringing me one of life's greatest surprises. It came by way of a hand-written letter which ran to three foolscap pages – it was from Sue! In fact she reminded me that ten weeks previously, I had visited her brother Tom in hospital in Dublin, and she went on to list the complaints from which he was suffering at that time. With all due respect to her, I would have needed to be in my third year of medical studies to understand the nature and complications of his illnesses! Next the letter astonishingly disclosed that on the morning after my visit, to the amazement of his family and the medical team, Tom began a slow but steady progress towards recovery and was discharged from hospital eight weeks after my visit! Sue waited a further two weeks, saw him settled down at home and then wrote to tell me the good news! Despite the evidence of my eyes, I could hardly believe what I was reading. Tom was home, well, and looking forward to spending Christmas with his wife and family. Then Sue added three glorious words, 'Praise the Lord'.

I was so stunned upon reading the letter that I remained motionless in my chair for some ten minutes or more. Surely Tom and his family could well identify the sentiments expressed in Scripture that often our lives can be compared to a bird who has escaped the snare of the fowler. Humanly speaking and from the medical point of view, Tom's life was drawing to a close when I visited him, with the prognosis confirming that he had no hope of recovery, but praise the Lord, God works in mysterious ways. Was there a direct intervention by the Supreme Being in Tom's illness? Am I describing a miracle? However, I do know this – I have recorded this tale as it unfolded before me, adding nothing to it or taking nothing from it. Therefore, all who read it must make up their own minds and answer these two questions for themselves. From my point of view, I have no difficulty at all as a Christian in recognising or accepting a miracle when I see it. As Christians, we are in the miracle business. I am only witnessing what the Lord said would happen when His disciples followed His way. It is as plain as daylight in the Gospel according to St Luke. There we read that Jesus Christ gave His disciples power and authority over all devils and to cure diseases, sending them out to proclaim the Kingdom of God and to heal. Furthermore we are told in that same Gospel that they set out, proclaimed the Good News and healed everywhere. Again I am not asking

166

you to take my word for it; read it for yourself in St Luke's Gospel chapter 9, verses 1–6. Exactly the same message and instructions can be confirmed in St Mark's Gospel chapter 16, verses 14–18. However, when you do look up these Scriptures, never forget that you are reading the Word of the Living God.

On that momentous early summer evening, unworthy as I am, I set out as Christ's man to visit Tom in hospital, to proclaim the Good News that Jesus Christ is Lord, and to heal him in His name. And it happened.

7

PERSONAL TESTIMONY OF A WOMAN AND A MAN

Personal Testimony of a Woman
On returning from holidays in late August 1993, opening my post, I read one of the most interesting letters I have ever received. It now gives me great pleasure to re-produce it exactly as it was written and I do so with the specific permission of the writer. As is my custom, I have omitted the address and changed the names and the locality shown in the original letter.

Dublin
21 August 1993

Dear Andy,

If I may be so bold to call you by your Christian name when you have never heard of me. My name is Sally O'Brien, married lady hitting 50, with three children – two boys and a girl. I don't quite know why I am writing to you except I have a great urge to do so. Although you don't know me I have heard of you over the years as I was once involved in Charismatic Renewal, which, looking back, was the most peaceful time of my life. In that time wonderful things happened; I was healed of a tumour in my jaw minutes before being operated on. My life was full of praise for the Lord and I was surrounded with loving friends, that is, until four years ago this coming September. You see Andy, it was then my faith was really put to the test. My father, with whom I had a bad relationship became ill; he was diagnosed with leukaemia. I felt I had to do something positive before he died so I took him

168

home to die. We had four wonderful weeks together, all the mis-understandings were put to rest and our love for each other became intense. When he died, I thought, 'The Lord has freed me from guilt; now I can get on with His work'. Alas, it was not to be. The shock of my father's death hit hard; rendered me inca-pable of doing anything. I could not get further than my front gate without panic, and so I gave up going anywhere. No prayer meetings. No Mass and I was a minister of the Eucharist. My prayers and praise seemed to go unheard. I was on the verge of suicide when a friend said, 'Get in touch with Andy O'Neill', so I wrote a note to you and received a short letter, wishing me well and a passage in Scripture. 'Big deal,' I said to myself. At that point I decided I didn't need anyone; God knew me and what I was going through, so it was in his hands to heal me. Needless to say, I was attending my doctor who, God love him, was at his wits end with me. I began going down hill rapidly. All my friends were gone except one. The wonderful priest and nuns I have known never called anymore. I felt deserted.

My health got worse and in February 1992 I collapsed. In March 1992 I entered hospital to have a hysterectomy. During all this time I still read Scripture and most important of all, fol-lowed my doctor's orders. I felt sure that my operation would solve all my health problems. Alas, once again, it was not to be. During the operation, problems arose, two fine veins were cut and I was bleeding to death. To save my life the doctors clamped off my kidney. Five days later, my kidneys collapsed and I was rushed to St Vincent's Hospital where the doctors decided that they would try to save my kidney by doing a re-implantation. The operation took six hours and the weeks that followed were a nightmare. During all that time, my only visitors were my fam-ily and my only friend, Liz. My moods were full of change, depressive fatigue, anger, low self-esteem and hostility. It was at this point that my friend asked would she get Andy O'Neill to come and pray with me. I agreed so she left word at the desk on her way out. I watched and waited over the following six weeks but no Andy, so I cursed your name with all the so-called do-gooders in Renewal. I vowed if I got back on my feet again I would never have anything to do with religious people, and so a year and six months later, my life remains so.

Yesterday, Saturday, while shopping, I decided to kill time by browsing over books in a new book shop. One book almost jumped at me; it was the only one left on the counter, The Power of Charismatic Healing, by you know who. I thought, 'Why is that man's name always popping up in my life? I don't know what he looks like or what he does other than visiting sick people, and anyhow he never answered my friend's call when I was at death's door last year in St Vincent's Hospital.' However, I could not take my eyes off your book, so I said a prayer. 'Lord, it is against my will, but if you want me to buy that book so be it.' When I took it to the lad at the counter, he said, 'Oh, Andy's book. I must get some more. It's a good read and it will not do you any harm!' So Andy, I am half way through it at present, hence the urge to write to you.

I have kept in close contact with my God and have written about thirty poems about my experiences and struggle. Still lurking in the back of my mind a voice keeps whispering, 'Take a step back into the world'. I am not a silly middle-aged woman! I know I still have a lot to offer, some purpose, be it very small. But what? I need advice and direction, also fellowship. Reading your book has lifted my spirit. I ask nothing of you except your prayers. I am still attending St Vincent's Hospital and always go into the little chapel to speak to God, for He has been my constant companion through my seemingly endless period of distress. My life is empty at the moment but I do feel that God has prepared me for something and so I watch and wait with great eagerness to start the second half of my life.

All I can say to you Andy is that I am sorry for ill-treating your name; it was unfair. God used my time in the desert to win me back, praise His holy name. By the way, I think I had better mention my poor husband, who has been such a brick through all my misfortunes, bless him. Please include him in your prayers, his name is James.

Yours sincerely
Sally O'Brien

PS It is now 5.30 pm Sunday and after praising God all day I have decided to go to Mass for the first time in months!

Shortly after receiving this letter I rang Sally, and when I introduced myself, she received my call with evident delight. Considering that she knew nothing of me other than what she gleaned from my books and I knew nothing of her other than what I learned from her letter, amazingly we chatted away like friends of a lifetime. In retrospect, all I remember of our conversation was that it was a laugh a minute session with no recrimination whatsoever; no explanations were offered or sought either. It was very evident also that Sally was rejoicing in the good health of mind and body, surrounded by a loving family, while being at peace again with the Lord. When inviting her to join us at our prayer meeting on some Wednesday evening in the near future, I borrowed a phrase from her letter suggesting that it might be as good a place as any to begin her, 'first steps back into the world'. For good measure I also advocated that she bring her long suffering husband with her! Sally's reaction typified her normality when she laughingly disclosed, 'That man came home from work yesterday and after dinner picked up your book; as a result he never spoke a word to me all evening! His silence continues tonight when he asked me not to bother him until he finishes it!' Finally, we shared a short prayer together and our call ended with Sally saying, 'You've made my day Andy. See you soon in "Avila"'.

Sally's experience and struggle could well have been an encounter with 'the dark night of the soul' syndrome, or it could simply be the tale of yet another female passing through the menopause. Yet again her troubles could have stemmed entirely from her illness. But whether or not her trial was rooted in one or in a variety of causes, Sally, by God's grace seemingly came successfully through her ordeal. For sure, she could also truly confirm that it is not a woman's world! Be that as it may, it has been proved over and over again in life that although the female of the species may bend, women rarely break. It is just as well that they don't, otherwise this old world of ours would most certainly disintegrate, despite all the strutting of the macho male!

It was also very consoling for me to learn that my book 'lifted Sally's spirit' – how simply she put her reflective intro-

spection! Actually, I'm invariably 'switched off' when someone endeavours to explain the different functions of the soul
and the spirit in humans. Maybe the simple truth of the matter
is that the action of the Holy Spirit (i.e. God's grace, God's gift)
on the soul of human beings results in a spiritual re-awaken-
ing, a desire of the creature to contact the Creator. Such a solution may not be that simplistic either as after all, men and
women are composed of body and spirit, irrespective of
whether or not some people reject the very notion of spirituality. Furthermore it is the universal experience of mankind that
all the creature comforts of this world do not or cannot minister to the spirit. Comforting also to know that the Spirit blows
where it wills. May it continue to blow in Sally's life and hopefully in mine too.

Personal Testimony of a Man
One morning, in November 1993, I had to 'rise and shine' before dawn to catch the 7.30 a.m. inter-city train from Dublin to
Cork, where I had a business appointment. On my arrival in
the southern capital, I hailed a taxi at the station and informed
the driver of my destination. He replied, 'Right, sir', opened
the passenger door, switched on the taxi meter and we were
away with the minimum of fuss on our drive across the city.
Predictably our chat initially ranged over subjects as inconse-
quential as the weather, politics and sport. I do remember
though asking him casually how he was doing in his business
and learned that he was making an adequate living, so much
so that he had lately moved to a new house, a venture very satisfying indeed, I gathered, to his wife and growing family too.
After a lapse of a few minutes my driver asked, 'What do you
do for a living?' and hearing that I was retired, instantly
observed, 'although I'm only in my late forties, the prospect of
retirement doesn't attract me in the slightest', adding, 'but I
must say you look very well on it. But tell me, how do you
manage your free time?' His tone of voice and expression
plainly indicated that he was at a complete loss to understand
how the golden years of life could be confronted, with the possibility of it bringing a fulfilling lifestyle being apparently

beyond comprehension. In short, I explained that much to my surprise, I found myself an author, having spent all my working life in insurance. The revelation interested him so much that it was easy to see that he was more than willing to listen to my story.

From my point of view it wasn't the time or the place, but he probed, 'What is the subject matter of your books?' and although I anticipated the question, I accepted that time was not on my side as we neared our destination. In reply, therefore, I gave him a politician's answer, saying, 'I doubt very much if you would be interested; it concerns a specific interest subject.'

Sticking to his guns he continued, 'What kind of specific interest?'

Maybe I should have kept my big mouth shut, I mused, but resignedly I replied, 'my books concern healing'.

Not satisfied, but warming to the challenge, he persisted, 'what kind of healing?'

I was concerned, so in the spirit of 'in for a penny, in for a pound', I proceeded to give him a general idea of the thrust of my books, outlining the details of one healing which is generally accepted as being a very dramatic incident indeed. He was admittedly amazed and reduced to silence when we came to our journey's end. He switched off the taxi meter, I paid my fare, gave him the title of my first book, with the publishers name and suggested that he read it some time. I opened the passenger door and when we shook hands, I was somehow moved to add, 'May the Good Lord bless, protect, heal and prosper you and your loved ones'. I then closed the car door, leaving a very lucid, intelligent, nobody's fool of a taxi-man seemingly very, very puzzled, to say the least of it.

I assumed that living almost 200 miles apart, we would never meet again, but, as seems par for the course in the Healing Ministry in which I find myself so unexpectedly involved, the Holy Spirit had other ideas, with the Third Person of the Most Holy Trinity being in no rush either to arrange our next meeting.

Some six months later, astonishingly and most unexpectedly, we met again when this Cork taxi-man, finding himself in Dublin's city centre, suddenly realised that as it was Wednesday evening, the 'Avila' Charismatic Renewal prayer meeting would be in session at that moment. Unsure of its location however, but being in the vicinity of Store Street police station, in an automatic reaction, he entered it and asked for directions. On learning that it was only a short drive away, he quit the police station, hailed a taxi and arrived at the crowded Carmelite Monastery Church at around 9 p.m. To his dismay, he could only squeeze into the rear passageway leading to the church where he stood listening for the first time to the sounds of a Charismatic Renewal prayer meeting, the whole experience producing mixed emotions of wonder and confusion in him. When the meeting ended, as I was leaving the Church, a man approached me and said, 'Mr O'Neill, I wouldn't expect you remember me – I'm the taxi-man who picked you up at the station in Cork last November.'

It was then 4 May 1994. My recall was instant (once he explained who he was!). I welcomed him and in some surprise asked, 'What are you doing here?' and listened as he explained that he had read my first and second books since meeting me, and actually began reading my third book that afternoon on his train journey from Cork en route to the UK. I couldn't help noticing, at first glance, that he seemed confused and deeply worried too, as simply and very humbly he asked for prayer. I honestly can't remember him mentioning why he wanted prayer, but not being in the counselling, prognosis or diagnosis disciplines, it was enough for me to realise that he was in need (aren't we all?), so I went into action seeking the blessing of God for him. Being conscious that the Lord was aware of his needs and that the taxi-man knew what he wanted, I readily accepted that I didn't need to know. I was carrying my Scripture so we held hands on it while I asked the Lord to bless him and his loved ones, in mind, body and spirit. The man seemed very moved by our three minute prayer session as we walked to the rear door of the church, and I listened as he explained that he was flying to the UK the following Saturday, having arranged to attend a football match on the Saturday of that week. Instantly, our conversation switched to soccer, but as I was called away from him, at that moment, we shook hands and wishing him good luck, I called out, 'Don't forget to send me a programme of the match', as he silently picked up his two travel bags and left.

Curiously enough, the strangeness of the encounter only dawned on me as I drove home. Frankly, I just couldn't understand why a man should set out from Cork on a Wednesday afternoon to attend a soccer match in the UK at the weekend, carrying two travel bags. For sure, he was going to be in time for the game! Humour aside though, it was all against the normal scene. Usually, soccer fans travel in groups, leave Ireland on the eve of matches, are exclusively attired in jeans, anoraks and sports shirts, with their cash out of sight in a money belt. In no way would any one of them be seen dead with a travel bag, never mind two travel bags! Furthermore, I couldn't figure out why he was off to the UK for what appeared to be a week's holiday while leaving his family at home alone. Maybe he had relatives in England or he could have had a business appointment or whatever. Nevertheless, the whole scenario looked quite odd to me. However, he had his own life and I hoped he wouldn't mess it up, but somehow, I knew his unplanned visit to 'Avila' on the eve of his trip, while at the very least it couldn't do him any harm, had the potential of bringing a miracle into his life, should he need it. After all, the Spirit blows where it wills.

On reaching home, however, the 'Avila' experience ended for me for another week, to begin all over again on the following Wednesday, should God spare me. Little did I know though that this taxi-man's saga was only beginning with the third instalment imminent. Days later, an outsize envelope arrived to me by post. I slit the package and in so doing opened yet another chapter of his story. The package contained a multi-coloured programme of the F.A. Carling premiership game featuring Newcastle United and Arsenal on 7 May 1994 at St James' Park, Newcastle-Upon-Tyne, a blown up A4 size photo of two men clasping hands in greeting plus a nine-page, closely written letter with the full name, address and telephone number of the sender. The communication was from my taxi-man friend in Cork and in this letter, all was revealed. Of the countless letters received at my home since I first went public on the Healing Ministry, I can unreservedly state that this one stunned me because of its total honesty, simplicity and utter humility. Not wishing to gild the lily further, I now have the pleasure of reproducing it exactly as it was written, doing so at the express wish and with the full authority of the sender. To preserve the principle of confidentiality, naturally, the names and location of the family concerned are fictional. This letter deeply affected me. Read on, and see how it affects you.

19 May 1994
(Sender's address)
Cork Telephone Number

Dear Andy,

If you can recall, I met you on Wednesday 4 May last in 'Avila'. I was there, having arrived in Dublin that evening from Cork on my way to see Newcastle United play their last league game on Saturday 7 May against Arsenal. Briefly, I have sup- ported Newcastle for the last 31 years and regularly went once during the season to see them play.

As I told you, I arrived in Dublin that evening and decided to try and find where the prayer meeting at 'Avila' was. I arrived at Store Street Garda Station and enquired -- to my surprise, Morehampton Road was not too far away, so I jumped into a taxi and arrived there just after nine o'clock. Having found my way into the monastery, I waited in the corridor outside the main door to the chapel. As 9.30 approached, I nervously waited, won- dering would this same Andy remember me picking him up some six months earlier in Cork railway station in a taxi to take him to a solicitor's office across the city.

As the people began to disperse and they passed me in the corridor, I could see that they were from all walks of life, young, old, and middle-aged and some with physical discomforts, but amazingly, all had this look of happiness and contentment on their faces, all seemed to have gotten this tremendous message and personal satisfaction from the meeting. This amazed me, a person who only occasionally had been to Mass in the last few years. Was I worthy of being there, I thought.

Well Andy, this is my story, which I am about to tell (sorry for the length of this letter).

I have been married for seventeen years to Terri and have four children (names and ages given). I have always loved soccer and going back six or seven years, I became more and more involved, both playing and managing a team. This left less and less time for my family and yes, you could say that a very selfish pattern in my life developed.

My wife Terri is a most loving and caring person (one in a million) and my four children love me very much. But I continued on my way (I'd just like to say that there was never any physical violence used by me within the family). I used to have a drink after training or after the match and this worsened, with me coming home later and later and on a regular basis, twice a week (Thursdays and either Saturdays or Sundays). Finally, going back around seven months ago, my wife Terri decided that it was about time to put her foot down, and tackled me. This I ignored, and continued, so she sought help from a Sister June, a Social Worker (qualified) who today, I have come to admire and respect deeply, a most wonderful person.

I came home one day from the taxi work to find a letter on the table addressed to me. In it, Sister June asked would I be willing to see her, as the break-up of my marriage was inevitable if I continued the way I was going. This I agreed to do and have been doing regularly with Terri, and both of us going separately as well. But unfortunately I have let Terri and my family down on a number of occasions and she had kept giving me another chance – the last occasion being my trip to Newcastle against her wishes. I did not expect her to be there when I got home, but she was, only to tell me that she could not take any more and that I had broken her heart for the last time.

During this time, I had read two of your books and was just finishing your third and, believing in fate, as I do, I knew some day that I would meet you again. Fate had it that I was reading your third book on my way to Dublin and I continued to read it in the plane over and back.

We went to Sister June last week for the inevitable. Sister June asked Terri to give me one last chance as she felt that we still had so much to offer. Terri said that she had heard it all before, broken promises and me not able to give my family the love and commitment they deserved. Andy, I never mentioned that I had met you on the Wednesday night in 'Avila'. The next few days passed and I was resigning myself to losing my family. No more than I deserved.

And you can imagine how I felt as I stood before you in 'Avila' with my hands on the Bible and the hurt I had done to the people who loved me most in this life. Yes, I'm not ashamed to admit I did not deserve another chance. But Andy, having met you on the fateful night, I recalled the words you had said to me, and asked was the Lord about to be merciful and forgive someone who had deeply hurt his family for so long in such a selfish way.

I awoke on Friday 13th, fearing the worst. I went down-stairs at nine o'clock – the kids were gone to school. Terri was having her breakfast. As I neared the tap to get a drink of water, for some unknown reason, Terri asked me did I want a cup of drinking chocolate (I have not drunk tea or coffee for 35 years).

I stood there in amazement. It was a month since she had last made me a cup. As I drank the chocolate, she said, 'Jimmy, can I tell you a story?' We had barely said a dozen words in the last month.

She said that on the previous night, late, around 12.30 (I was in bed alone), when she was hanging out some washing on the line in the still of the night, this tremendous feeling came over her which she could not explain and remained with her throughout the night as she did not sleep very much. She asked me from the bottom of her heart would I be prepared to save the marriage and all concerned. I told her to sit down, as I had some-thing to tell her. Then I told her about meeting you in Dublin on the Wednesday night prior to flying to Newcastle the following day and what you had said. Andy, she is convinced our Lord, One who is so merciful, got through to her.

Well, our present position – we are still attending Sister June, both together and separately. Terri feels it will take a long

178

time for herself to heal – her broken heart, so selfishly shattered.

Andy, I have asked her to read your books which she is about to do. Also, I've picked up in the taxi a few people who have some sickness or personal trauma in their lives, and I have asked them to consider reading your books which so many people have been privileged to read as I see it. I will be coming to 'Avila' at a later date – I will let you know when if you wish – hopefully with Terri.

I cannot find words to describe how much I am in debt to you and the Lord who is so merciful. I have gotten the chance I thought I'd never get. For this, I am truly grateful. May you continue spreading the Word of the Lord and the Healing Ministry that goes with it. Bless you always.

Should or when you decide to write the next book and you want to include my story, you have my utmost permission.

Yours sincerely,

Jimmy (surname)

PS Andy, I'm enclosing a picture of the former Newcastle player, 'Mr X' who, on hearing I had come from Ireland and was anxious to meet him, got off his sick bed and met me. I waited over 20 years to meet him. He played in the 1974 Cup final against Liverpool.

As you can see, from the photo, he doesn't look too well. He's having tests at present for some complaint in his stomach which they think is cancerous – a person I found who faced up to his illness with great dignity and bore no ill-feelings to anyone nor looked for sympathy. A most remarkable and the most sincere person in football I've met. I'm a good judge of people and had I met him a few years ago, I still would have come to this conclusion. Andy, is it possible to keep him in your prayers, and would the Lord keep him close to His heart? If you're ever coming to Cork in the future Andy, please let me know. I hope you enjoy the programme you asked for. Sorry for the length of the letter. Do feel free to write or phone any time.

I read and re-read this letter when I received it and then sat quietly for some fifteen minutes recalling when I last saw

Jimmy and how bemused, bothered and bewildered he was, leaving 'Avila', with a travel bag in each hand, walking out into the night alone. Perusing the match programme, I vividly remembered too watching that particular game, the last one of the season, late on the Saturday night on BBC TV's *Match of the Day* series (which programme I watched for many years). I know now that Jimmy was among the chanting, singing fans roaring on the home side's 2-0 victory over their traditional London, age-old sporting rivals. While in no way did I wish to involve myself in Jimmy's marital problems (the Healing Ministry give me more than sufficient challenges), I was naturally consoled with the knowledge that a qualified social worker, God bless her, was in action with the family. With the volume of mail dictating I daren't leave correspondence pile up, I dashed off a quick note to Jimmy, thanked him for thinking of me with the gift of a match programme, frankly admitted that his letter had 'bowled me over', and promised to give him a ring at the weekend, taking advantage of the concessionary trunk call charges operating on these days.

Honouring my bond then on the following Saturday, I rang Jimmy's home, introduced myself and received a royal welcome. His doom and gloom days were plainly over, I perceived, so much so that in football terminology, he could safely be described as being 'over the moon'! First, I learned that his multi-paged letter had a difficult birth; he began writing it on one night at 11.45 p.m. and didn't finish until 3.45 a.m! Second, he explained that he was now at peace with himself, had already begun plans to wind down his taxi business, it being too time-consuming, and had made the first moves to go into other business activities. Then, for me, came the icing on the cake when he hollered, 'Terri! Terri! Andy is on the phone', and how lovely it was to also hear her say how delighted she was when my letter arrived. I learned too that the entire family had celebrated a joyful day together on the occasion of the First Holy Communion of one of their four children on that Saturday.

Eventually Jimmy broke into the conversation, disclosing that he and Terri were concerned about the health of one of their children who was due in hospital over the coming week for a scan. When I volunteered to pray for the healing of their little girl, Jimmy instantly handed the phone to his spouse and both listened as I went straight to the Lord with the problem. From my books, Jimmy was familiar with the Scripture that I invariably recommend to parents for the healing of offspring and he also recalled the prayer I add, based on that word of the Gospel of St Luke in chapter 2. Therefore, I pointed them towards that daily routine, and we ended by saying the Gloria together. I made very sure to emphasise too that they pause for a split second at the door of the hospital to leave the Lord go before them, on their daughter's admission day. The results when people do so speak for themselves, for which we give the glory to God. They both thanked me with Jimmy signing off saying, 'I hope to attend "Avila" again very soon, Andy, but next time Terri will be with me!' It was music to my ears.

When the call ended I was satisfied that the signs were at least hopeful for the renewal of their marriage, although I recognised that Terri's hurt would not be healed instantly; the scars of their trip to hell and back couldn't go deeper. Terri, by her stand, had put justice before love and in doing so opted to support the right ordering of the society where we all live. It's now down to Jimmy to dedicate himself to the task of rehabilitating his spouse's trust in him. In football jargon, from his point of view, it's all there to play for now. By God's grace and the power of the Holy Spirit, may he win the hand of that 'one woman in a million' (as he so aptly describes her in his memorable letter to me) for the second time in his life.

Jimmy's story could well have a Somerset-Maugham type twist in the plot involving that good servant of Newcastle United who in the years gone by brought glory days to that world famous north-east of England football club. During his visit, Jimmy made it his business to seek out 'Mr X', call to his home and, although the former football hero is now seriously ill and was resting after medical treatment, he got out of his bed to greet Jimmy, their visit lasting $1^1/2$ hours! I suggested that Jimmy send my first book to his sick friend; and who knows, should he do so, maybe it will be the first step in another dramatic healing. After all, healing by the power of the Holy Spirit is as wide as life itself.

Interestingly, Jimmy's unplanned visit to 'Avila' was followed by dramatic events in his marriage relationship. It is worth noting too that within days of praising God in the Carmelite Monastery, he was moved to visit the sick during his stay in Newcastle. It should not be forgotten either that it was Jesus Christ Himself who said, 'When you do it to these, the least of my brethren, you do it to me', with Jimmy doing just that when he called to 'Mr X's' home. In performing these twin actions of praising God and visiting the sick, whether or not he is aware of it, Jimmy fulfilled the whole law of the prophets. When Christians do so, they should expect miracles. Why not, for with God, nothing is impossible, as the Good Book proclaims.

Jimmy's letter, football programme and blown up photo of his visiting the sick have all been added to my personal Healing Ministry memorabilia. As I am wont to observe, should those that I meet through the Charismatic Renewal prayer movement not be generous and sincere people, then I can throw my hat at trying to find such people anywhere else on earth.

EPILOGUE

These two personal testimonies herald the end of my fourth book on healing, which, like my three previous works, is packed with good news. Consequently, a question that I am often asked is, 'Why is it that you constantly experience these varied signs, wonders and comforting happenings?' My initial response is, 'Maybe I see healings because I very much want to!' Believe me, this is not a simplistic reply to be dismissed out of hand either; rather it is a basic characteristic, I believe, essential for those who seek to enter or find themselves in the Healing Ministry of the Holy Church. I realise too that from the very first moment of my consciousness, I always deeply loved people. I wanted to be with them, was with others, sought out their company and found the utmost satisfaction expressing myself with people. I was never cut out to be a loner, that's for sure! Apart altogether from religion it always disturbed me to see people unhappy or suffering, which seemingly fuelled a natural desire in me to offer whatever help I could. Similarly, deep down, I was never drawn to acquire the 'killer instinct' so widely promoted by coaches in sport and by entrepreneurs in business, and whenever I was a winner, while thoroughly enjoying the experience and fruits of victory, I was always concerned for and conscious of the losers around me.

Naturally then, when I came to take a serious adult look at the faith I inherited (Christianity of the Catholic variety!) the second of the two great commandments confirmed by the Lord's New Commandment simply gave religious effect to what seemed normal behaviour for me. In retrospect then, with this outlook entering the Society of St Vincent de Paul and from thence the Healing Ministry of the Holy Church via Charismatic Renewal (as described in my first book, *The Power of Charismatic Healing*) it would seem to have been a very predictable progression – assisted by God's grace too, I hasten to add! I now admit too that when the gift of healing first manifested itself in my life, I frankly didn't quite know what to do with it or how to handle it but the whole problem was solved by the 'Avila' experience. Being led by a combination of circumstances and again by God's grace, to the Carmelite Monastery in my adopted city of Dublin was most certainly instrumental in comfortably fitting activity in the Healing Ministry into my life without unduly disturbing my family life, business career, sporting or cultural pursuits. In other words, the duties of my state of life were never threatened or restricted by such exertions. Without a shadow of a doubt then, I can confirm it was God's people in 'Avila' who encouraged me to continue to exercise the Lord's gift of healing, while more importantly, ensuring that it was rooted in common sense.

I am also convinced that I experience healings so constantly because of my regular attendance at the 'Avila' prayer meeting where exceptional spiritual activity is generated and released by the action of some hundreds of people exercising their faith. Furthermore, realising that spiritual warfare exists, I would not dare to be active, alone, in the Healing Ministry without the support, goodwill and protection afforded by a praising and praying community. Being conscious then that Christians are opposed by 'principalities and powers', I therefore firmly believe that those who engage in the discipline of the laying on of hands without the back-up of an active prayer group, expose themselves to unacceptable risks.

Of primary importance too in discovering why I witness healings is, I believe, the nature of the 'Avila' prayer meeting. There, each Wednesday evening, the Lord is worshipped exclusively in i) praise, ii) tongues, iii) prophecy, iv) the word, v) teaching, vi) personal testimony, and vii) orthodox, worldwide, traditional Charismatic Renewal methods of worship, all so familiar to God's Chosen people, the Jews, for so many centuries while being passed on faithfully from Apostolic times to this age. Therefore, all efforts to introduce other devotions and spiritual exercises into the one hour and twenty minutes of the communal act of worship in the 'Avila' meeting are firmly and regularly discouraged. Being the largest weekly Charismatic Renewal prayer meeting in Ireland ensures that a succession of people are drawn to that meeting who desire to promote many other Catholic devotions. Such people usually have neither knowledge of, interest in, or enthusiasm for Renewal; basically their target is the congregation. Understandably, those with bees in their bonnets take every opportunity to fatten those bees so that when the congregation in 'Avila' is invited to add to or substitute for the seven elements of Charismatic Renewal worship a particular exercise, be it a novena, veneration of a saint, activity associated with a shrine at home or abroad or whatever, this invitation is invariably declined.

Time and time again, members of the 'Avila' core group find themselves explaining that although there are innumerable ways to the Lord, those who gather at a Charismatic Renewal prayer meeting have chosen a particular route. While a win is a win is a win is a familiar maxim in sport, so in the spiritual life, prayer is prayer is prayer, but the 'Avila' congregation on one specific evening each week expresses its spirituality in the Renewal way and consequently expect those who attend to respect that decision. After all, there are six other evenings in the week for advocates to promote other devotional exercises should they so desire! However, I am convinced that when the Lord is praised in the seven-fold Renewal manner, healing tends to surface regularly and is particularly frequently evident at the laying on of hands when the communal worship ends. The 'Avila' Wednesday evening power house of prayer must therefore be a major factor in determining the reason for the healings I experience, and is a conclusion totally confirmed by the Acts of the Apostles where we read of the disciples praising God and then healing the sick. In no way were these signs and wonders restricted either.

In analysing healing even in a rudimentary manner, the method of praying with those in need (is there any other kind of person in the world?) is I believe of fundamental importance. When I was honoured with an invitation to join the prayer team at 'Avila', I was immediately exposed to a distinctive prayer style. First, I learned to quickly establish the nature of the healing I required. Second, I was made aware of the solemnity of the laying on of hands, a custom rich in tradition and practised by Christ and his Apostles. Third, I recognised that the members of the prayer team were quick, decisive and direct in prayer; accepting that Jesus Christ healed with a word and a touch, their prayers were never long-winded. Fourth, it was plainly evident too that the prayer team prayed with people, never over them, acknowledging their role as labourers in the Healing Ministry. Fifth, they always asked the Lord to take authority over situations, never took personal responsibility over these circumstances, ruled out counselling, accepted medicine and the laying on of hands as complementary disciplines while unhesitatingly and positively seeking total healing. Considering the Word of God is the foundation of the Charismatic Renewal movement, as could be expected then, the prayers at the laying on of hands were exclusively based on Scripture. Finally, when witnessing instant healings or hearing of miracles reported from previous sessions, the prayer team immediately gave the glory to God. He alone is the Lord. These praying skills learned by me and finely honed by *populi Dei* in 'Avila', plus the discipline of the laying on of hands, together with the weekly communal worship of the Lord in the Renewal manner have resulted in healings galore. I realise too that I am very privileged to work at the coal face of the Church's Healing Ministry where I freely and regularly give part of my spare time ministering to the needy when invited to do so. At the same time I fully appreciate that the significance of those who witness healing when they engage in the laying on of hands, is of no consequence whatsoever – is neither here nor there. The power to heal is the Lord's alone; the glory must always be given to Him.

So much for the theory of healing, but believe me, if I did not witness the power of the Word in action in the real world where I exist, then my being actively involved the Healing Ministry would be a colossal waste of effort. At the same time I can't offer any explanation why countless prayers of petition go unanswered and unheeded despite the Word of God expressly indicating that anything asked of the Lord in Jesus' name would be granted; nor can anyone else enlighten me either in this regard. One may also well ask, 'How do you account for so many lives unfulfilled and strewn with broken dreams?' Again, despite the logic of my arguments and endeavours to tease out the workings of the Church's Healing Ministry, I'm as much in the dark as the next person. As Christians live by the mystery of faith not by fact, there is then no more frustrating exercise in life than dealing with mystery. Consolingly though, despite the darkness, in spite of the hopelessness, in the midst of torrents of helplessness, even in the depths of the numbness of human agony in the lives of those written off as losers in worldly terms, amazingly a ray of sunshine suddenly, stunningly and unpredictably, transforms desperately forlorn personal circumstances. The midnight sun does shine.

ON A WARM, BALMY summer Wednesday afternoon, driving home after a leisurely round of golf (one of the joys of retirement!) on the spur of the moment, I called into St Vincent's Hospital to visit Mike. I found him in the TV lounge, alone, having a cup of tea, aimlessly gazing at a kid's cartoon. I knew he had been hospitalised for some five weeks, yet there he was, down and out. 'How are things, Mike?' I enquired. I wouldn't blame him should he have answered, 'ask a stupid question, Andy, and you'll get a stupid answer!' but he remained silent, leading me to assume that he had received bad news, health wise. We just sat together for a minute or two as I strove to be physically present to him, when quietly he revealed that he was being discharged next day. 'That's good news,' I responded, but apparently it wasn't, as in a few cryptic sentences, Mike outlined his circumstances. It proved to be an unrelieved doomsday scenario.

Quickly, I learned that Mike was aged 55, married, separated and living in a 'bad flat' (his words). He hadn't contacted his wife for years and his two daughters had emigrated. A manual worker, he was unemployed with a physical condition now indicating that he would hardly work again. Considering that his flat was empty for almost two months, his doctors would not consent to him returning to his bed-sit equipped only with an open fire place and a breakfast cooker. The possibility of a damp bed, his very apparent difficulties in organising fuel, food and laundry arrangements in advance of his discharge date, had prompted the medical authorities to find alternative accommodation for him in a nursing home for two weeks. Meanwhile, the social services had been alerted and hopefully some solution would be found to ease Mike's culture shock. The prospect of leaving centrally heated surroundings where hot meals were served, plus a spotlessly clean and comfortable bed simply terrified him. No wonder Mike was slumped in a chair, like nobody's child. Instantly I resolved to contact the hospital's Social Work Department and offer the assistance of the Society of St Vincent de Paul in Mike's situation, but before I could mention it, the urgent ringing of a bell announced the end of visiting time. We stood up and shook hands when suddenly I decided to take a spiritual leap in the dark. Keeping his hand in mine, I traced the sign of the cross on it with my thumb and heard myself say, 'Mike, my wish is that you and your wife may get together again. How it will happen I don't know – God knows. May you then enjoy the security, freedom and happiness of marriage, as Delia and I have, for well over 40 years now.' I released his hand and headed for the hospital exit. Mike was dumbfounded and while I didn't look back, I would have bet dollars to doughnuts that he was stuck to the floor at that moment.

Irrespective of the ways of the world, life goes on, I realised as I drove home knowing I had a date to praise the Lord in 'Avila' on that same evening. On the following morning, immediately after breakfast, my phone rang. It was Helen, a nurse in St Vincent's Hospital, a friend of the family, ringing me from her home, having come off night duty; she was attached to Mike's ward! Helen excitedly exclaimed, 'Mike was telling me that you prayed with him yesterday afternoon. Well Andy, last evening he had a surprise – his wife and her sister arrived at his bedside!' In awe I listened as Helen revealed that Mike's spouse, out of the blue, had invited him to return home! Apparently, within minutes, they had agreed to give their marriage a second chance, and on that Thursday afternoon, instead of heading for a nursing home and a very

188

uncertain future, Mike found himself in the passenger seat of a car with his wife, returning to the home he hadn't seen for five years!

Helen delightedly went on to describe how on that Wednesday evening, when visiting time ended, Mike escorted his two visitors to the hospital exit, before hurrying back to the ward to spread the good news to his fellow patients and nursing staff. Actually it was difficult to get Mike to bed as he sat in the nurses station, drinking innumerable cups of tea, talking non-stop, quite unable to come to terms with his unbelievable news. Helen remarked that he was like a man who had just won millions in a lottery! Unhesitatingly too he accepted the direct connection between the prayer and a handclasp only hours previously in the hospital TV lounge with the almost instant but miraculous turn-around in his fortunes. How much closer to a miracle can one get? Nobody witnessed our 30 second impromptu prayer; nor would anyone ever have heard of it unless Mike told of the happening. Not alone did he give the glory to God for the remarkable event by giving widespread testimony to all and sundry in the hospital, he also admitted a whole new world had been opened for him on learning from Helen for the first time ever of the Charismatic Renewal movement, 'Avila' and my books on healing. Astonishingly, Mike found that he had endless questions to ask concerning the power of the Lord to heal through the laying on of hands.

For my part, I instantly accepted the direct connection between Mike's story and the 'Avila' prayer meeting as it was precisely when the congregation in 'Avila' was praising God that Mike's wife walked back into his life! And didn't he need her! Right through the Scriptures it is evident that when God's people obeyed the Word they were deeply blessed by the Lord. Similarly in this day and age those who attend Charismatic Renewal meetings are also obeying the word as explicitly expressed in the Letter to the Hebrews chapter 10, verse 25 and therefore they, their loved ones and friends should expect to receive abundant blessings. Expressed in the language of the Holy Spirit this is nothing less than 'walking in expectant faith'. After Mike's mind-blowing experience on the eve of his

189

discharge from hospital no one would argue against such conclusions, that's for sure!

Interestingly too, shortly before my Wednesday afternoon visit to Mike, I received a prophecy as follows. 'Never, never, never look on the dark side of anything.' Being hopeful, joyful, consoling and encouraging, it certainly qualified as valid Charismatic Renewal prophecy which excludes all doom and gloom utterances. While that same word goes to the heart of positive thinking too, on many occasions in life as everyone knows, a positive outlook alone, does not suffice. However that particular ten word prophecy, to a believer, more importantly is based on the teaching of Jesus Christ, 'I am the light of the world', therefore it reflects the limitless power possessed by God alone. Maybe it's a good note on which to bring my book to a close. This prophecy sums up too the philosophy of those who work in the Healing Ministry. The labourers of the Lord in the vineyard of the needy most certainly are not engaged in as useless an exercise as whistling in the wind. Rather they see and want to see the glory of God revealed in startlingly joyful miracles, many times happening before their very eyes. Despite blighted hopes, unfulfilled ambitions, the riddle of the universe and broken dreams, it is still a wonderful world. It has to be – it's God's very own creation, a faint image of the glory awaiting His faithful people, in a future home where eye has not seen nor ear heard nor has it entered into the hearts of man or woman to conceive what God has in store for those who love Him – and who return that love by ministering to others.

The bottom line for each individual everywhere in the Charismatic Renewal prayer movement is to achieve personal salvation, by God's grace. May that priceless miracle be granted to all who read this book too – and to the man who wrote it!

Praised be Jesus Christ.